Bobbin Lace Making

Pamela Nottingham September 1986.

Bobbin Lace Making

Pamela Nottingham

B.T. Batsford Ltd, London

Also by Pamela Nottingham and published by Batsford:
The Technique of Bobbin Lace *(1976)*
The Technique of Torchon Lace *(1979)*
The Technique of Bucks Point Lace *(1981)*

*I appreciate very much the help and encouragement
that I receive from my husband, Arthur Johnson
and again thank him for his patience and skill in
producing all the illustrations. Through the craft of
bobbin lace making I have made many friends, in
Britain and overseas, and I should like to thank
them for their interest and enthusiasm.*

ISBN 0 7134 4132 1

Filmset by Servis Filmsetting Ltd, Manchester
and printed in Great Britain by
The Anchor Press Ltd
Tiptree, Essex
for the publishers B.T. Batsford Ltd
4 Fitzhardinge Street London W1H 0AH

Contents

Preface

The planning and preparation of an introductory book has given me particular pleasure as I am delighted by the increasing number of people who learn and practise the craft. In the past, bobbin lace making was a cottage industry and women worked long hours to augment the meagre family income. Today lace making provides the opportunity to extend an interest in textile crafts; some people wish to work at traditional patterns whilst others will use the techniques to create something original and exciting.

When making lace it is important to reason why, to see the direction in which threads travel, to make stitches automatically and then to work at repetitive patterns until reference to instruction is no longer necessary. This seems hard, and it is a challenge to learn, but one must develop a sound understanding and logical approach. Chapters 4, 6 and 7 give the methods for three different types of lace. The basic stitches are common to all, but the laces are made quite differently. Tape lace is an excellent introduction and will provide an outlet for enthusiastic yet inexperienced workers who want to make their own patterns. Torchon lace is geometric, easily understood and offers the opportunity to develop good method. Plaited laces have more freedom in design and provide a useful background for the making of mats, motifs and eventually collars and other large articles. Braids and trims in chapter 8 are quick and straightforward, drawing on simple techniques from all types. In each chapter the patterns are graded and offer new techniques. A variety of thread is used, the finer patterns require the same knowledge but more patience and skill to work with recommended thread. The last chapter is the real challenge with twenty patterns within the scope of the lace maker who has mastered the earlier chapters. They have been selected for quick completion and are suitable for gifts or personal use.

Equipment can be obtained without great expense, a pillow can be made quite easily or purchased from a specialist supplier. Examples of modern bobbins are illustrated in the frontispiece. Many are elaborate, showing the skill of the wood turner and these will enhance a pillow and delight the owner. Simple functional bobbins are available for the person new to the craft. Recently, one skilled bobbin maker, to cope with the huge demand, has had plastic bobbins made to his own specification. Many lace makers avoid plastic as out of keeping with the craft, but these are quite exceptional in use and appearance and worthy of consideration. It is advisable to purchase the minimum of equipment until one has the opportunity to see what is available.

In England a lace guild has been formed and this acts as a focal point for those interested in all types of lace. In the United States of America the International Old Lacers Inc. has a similar function. Smaller associations are developing in other countries. In the British Isles there are meetings – Lace Days – when as many as two hundred lace makers attend. Suppliers are present and this is an ideal chance to see and discuss the range of equipment and materials, and to meet fellow enthusiasts. Obviously, the development of the craft and the depth of study are at the discretion of the individual. Lace making has much to offer, enjoyed by people of all ages, it is an absorbing occupation, full of fascination and variety.

1 Equipment and Materials

Equipment and materials are obtainable easily and without great expense for the person who wishes to try the craft of bobbin lace making. Initially acquire only the minimum, because with a little knowledge and experience and the opportunity to see the wide range of pillows and bobbins available one will select according to personal preference. There are many stockists of lace making equipment throughout the country and many people have taken up the craft of bobbin making as a full-time occupation. Some offer a mail order service which includes advice for the inexperienced purchaser. Essential equipment is listed below and advice given on the use of temporary substitutes until one is certain of continuing the craft. However, it must be remembered that these are *not* as satisfactory, nor as easy to use as the recommended items.

Pillow

These vary in size and shape according to their country of origin. Pillows in use in England at the present time include those shown in illustration 1. In the past they were stuffed with straw but today other modern materials are used. The requirements of the pillow are threefold:

(i) It must be very hard so that the pins remain upright and will not move as the lace is worked.

(ii) There must be a flat area to support the bobbins with sufficient space to allow the lace maker to move them easily. The flat pillow and the French pillow have ample space and are most convenient for the inexperienced worker. Use of the bolster and square pillows requires more practice, but these were traditionally used in England when lace making was a cottage industry.

(iii) A slope is necessary to ensure good tension. Lace is made at the top of the roller on the French

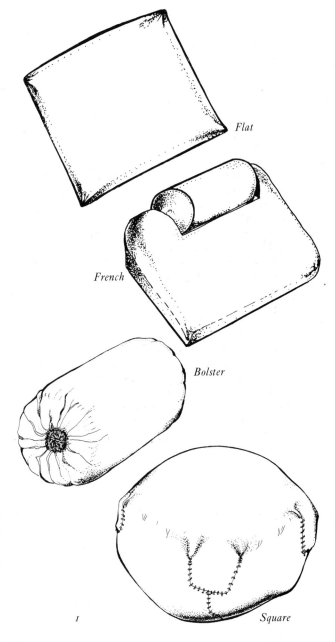

Flat

French

Bolster

Square

1

7

pillow and the threads fall down to the area where the bobbins are handled, the weight of the bobbin makes the thread taut and the lace firm. The flat pillow derives its name from the fact that it is made from a flat board, but when stuffed with straw it slopes towards the edges. Good tension is maintained on a bolster pillow as the threads fall from the work. Bolster and square pillows are excellent when large numbers of bobbins are used. A wide variety of pillows are available, or you can make one quite quickly.

To make a flat pillow

You need a piece of plywood approximately 350 × 400mm (14 × 16 inches) and one metre of strong cotton or linen fabric, preferably dark blue or green. These colours are traditional and more restful to the worker's eyes than bright colours and patterns. Successful pillows have been made using a 14 inch cake board of the drum type as a base, hardboard is not recommended as it bends when stuffed with straw. Illustration 2: place the board on the fabric as shown and draw a pencil line on the fabric along the 350mm (14 inch) edges of the board. Machine stitch along these lines to form a bag. Cut away the excess half metre of fabric, turn the bag so that the raw edges are inside and slide the board in. It must fit *very* closely, a loosely fitting bag will take a lot of filling and it will be impossible to achieve a hard pillow. Straw or hay, preferably chopped to 75mm (3 inch) lengths, is packed in *one* side tightly. The use of a wooden spoon or piece of wood is recommended to get the filling into the corners. Oversew the remaining edges.

After several months of use it may be necessary to re-open the pillow and add more straw, alternatively, a pleat may be made at one end to reduce the size of the bag. If new calico is used, this can be dampened when the pillow is complete, any shrinkage will reduce the bag and harden the pillow. The pillow must be dried very thoroughly afterwards. The spare fabric is cut in half and both pieces hemmed on all sides for use as cover cloths. Many lace makers are making excellent pillows using a piece of 75mm (3 inch) thick polystyrene (shaved down on the edges) covered with carpet underlay, smooth side uppermost. The underlay is slashed at the corners as necessary to get a close fit and held in position by the closely fitting bag. Only an underlay with a firm woven backing is successful.

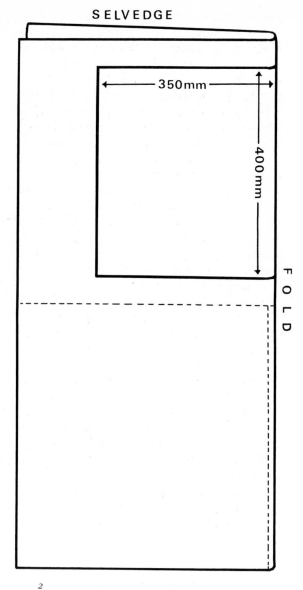

SELVEDGE

350mm

400mm

FOLD

2

Bobbins

No pattern in this book requires more than fifty bobbins. (Refer to illustration 3.) Most lace makers in England prefer the East Midlands bobbins, probably because they are attractive to look at and a wide variety may be collected. They are slim and take up little space on the pillow, the beads prevent them from rolling and help to keep them in position, for this reason they are very suitable for the inexperienced lace maker. The South Bucks bobbin is larger but not suited to the flat pillow as it requires more space than the East Midlands bobbin and will roll, causing the thread to unravel. The French bobbin with its large neck is useful to the student who wishes to work with a wide range of threads.

The requirements of the bobbin are threefold, firstly a neck on which to wind thread, secondly a convenient shank which can be held easily and thirdly weight to keep the thread taut. The weight in the South Bucks and French bobbins lies in the thickness of the wood, but in the East Midlands bobbin depends on the beads or spangle. Simple wooden or plastic bobbins are available and it is usual for the lace maker to add the spangle. Any glass or ceramic beads are satisfactory, wooden and plastic beads are too light in weight.

To make the spangle take a 70mm ($2\frac{1}{2}$ inch) length of brass or copper wire (picture hanging wire is readily obtainable and can be unravelled) and thread it through the hole at the bottom of the bobbin. Thread beads on each end and then hook the ends around each other and twist each end back on itself. Cut off excess wire; depending on the holes in the beads, the wire join may partly disappear inside the hole. The traditional arrangement of beads is shown in illus. 3. Old bobbins are highly prized antiques but the craft of bobbin making has returned and bobbins fashioned in wood and bone with pewter, wire and personal inscriptions surpass in skill those made in the nineteenth century.

Bobbin case

To keep pairs of bobbins ready for use the case is not essential but very useful and can be made using illustration 4 as a guide.

Pins

Brass or stainless steel pins will not corrode and are therefore advisable. Berry pins and hat pins are useful to hold bobbins in position on the pillow but are *never* used in the pricking.

3

Pin vice

This will hold a no. 8 Sharps sewing needle and is used to prick holes in card to make the lace patterns. There are a wide variety of pin vices available but the author recommends the small brass model, known to the jeweller and silversmith as a 'broacher holder'. It is comparatively inexpensive, easy to use and the needles remain firm when the collet is screwed up by hand. It is shown in illustration 5. Temporarily the lace maker can make a pricker by forcing the eye end of a no. 8 needle into bottle cork.

Pricking board

A piece of polystyrene or a cork mat is required. Ascertain that it is thick enough to prevent the needle from marking the surface underneath. Drawing pins are used to fasten the pattern to the board.

Pricking card

A thick brown glazed card is obtainable from suppliers. It is absolutely essential to use this to achieve good results. However, as a temporary measure, two pieces of a dark coloured manilla card can be glued together. White lace thread will show up and simplify lace making if a dark coloured card and a pillow covered in dark fabric are used.

Thread

The lace maker becomes bewildered by the range of threads offered today. Linen thread is preferable as it is durable and produces a firm and attractive lace. However, it is very expensive and most people will use cotton thread for practice work. In the past, linen, cotton and silk were available and lace was made in black, white and ecru. Today, it is usual to retain the traditional threads when working the old patterns. However, if the lace maker adapts the old techniques and develops a modern approach to the craft, there is opportunity to make use of many threads and yarns, both man-made and natural fibres, in a wide range of colours. The main problems that arise when using unconventional threads result from twist and resilience. A highly twisted thread, e.g. crochet cotton, may appear harsh and uneven when additional twisting takes place as the bobbins are moved. A thread with little

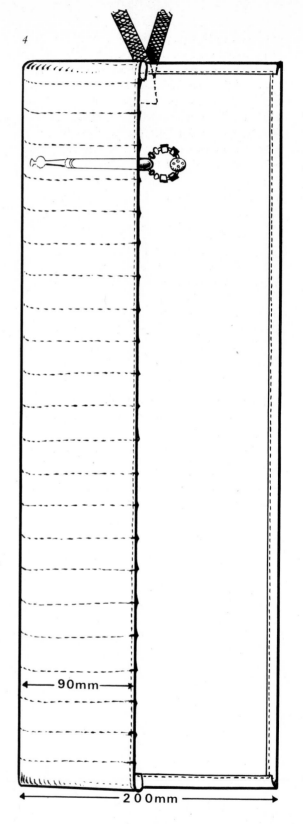

90mm

200mm

twist appears to separate, is untidy and may break easily. Wool and some of the man-made fibres have some elasticity and do not give clear, crisp results. To learn the basic techniques quickly, to achieve good tension and stitches that are seen clearly the use of cotton or linen is recommended for the inexperienced lace maker. The patterns in this book use a variety of threads but Fils a Dentelles and Pearl cotton no. 12 are used for the easier patterns. For those lace makers who rely on a mail order service, the following information should prove useful.

DMC Fils a Dentelles no. 70   106 yards per ball
Pearl cotton no. 12   130 yards per ball
        no. 8   95 yards per ball
        no. 5   53 yards per ball
Retors D'Alsace no. 30   880 yards per reel
        no. 50   1480 yards per reel
Dewhurst's Sylko no. 40   100 yards per reel
Twilley's Staylite   50 gram ball
Staylite and Pearl cotton no. 5 are used for gimp threads only in the patterns given here, but may be useful for experimental work.

Threads which appear to be similar in texture and thickness may work up very differently, the lace may appear thick and close or very fine and lacelike. Threads are grouped for similarity, but this can act only as a guide.

A   Pearl cotton no. 12, Bockens linen no. 35, Campbells linen no. 50.
B   Fils a Dentelles no. 70, Bockens linen nos. 50/60, Campbells linen no. 70.
C   Retors D'Alsace no. 30, Bockens linen no. 90, Campbells linen no. 100, Dewhursts Sylko no. 40 (easily obtainable for colour work).
D   Retors D'Alsace no. 50, English Sewing Co. Unity nos. 100/150

Crochet hooks

Fine steel crochet hooks are required to join tape lace and to complete motifs and mats.

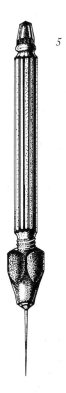

5

2 Preparation

To wind bobbins

When beginning a pattern, bobbins are used in pairs, knots and thread ends are avoided by putting thread on bobbins as follows:

(i) Hold the bobbin in the left hand and the thread in the right hand.

(ii) Wind the thread over and away in a clockwise direction as shown in illus. 6. Wind evenly as much thread as possible onto this bobbin. Cut the thread.

6

(iii) Take a second bobbin in the left hand and wind half of the thread from the first bobbin onto the second. This may seem tedious but thread will tangle and knot if any length is left unwound.

(iv) Refer to illustration 7 and make a hitch on the neck of each bobbin. Allow about 150mm (6 inches) of thread between the bobbins.

(v) Temporarily wind the thread round the neck of one of the bobbins, place in a bobbin case or put two or three pairs together with a rubber band.

To prepare the pricking

(i) If working on graph paper, mark where the holes are to be made, using a sharp pointed pencil according to instructions.

If the pattern is to be copied from a book make an accurate tracing or take a photocopy.

(ii) Cut a piece of card slightly larger than the pattern, place the pattern on top of the card and fix firmly to the pricking board, using drawing pins at the four corners.

(iii) Screw the needle into the pin vice, allowing 12mm ($\frac{1}{2}$ inch) to protrude. Hold in a vertical position and prick through the markings accurately.

(iv) Check carefully to ascertain that all holes have been put in. It is impossible to make the lace if holes are missing. Remove the drawing pins and the top copy.

(v) On the card, draw in any markings using a pencil. Mark in permanently using Indian ink. Exact marking is essential as this is the guide when making the lace. Ball point pens are unsuitable as the ink rubs off and discolours the lace.

To prepare the pillow

Place the card pricking on the pillow and secure with lace pins at the corners. Take a hemmed cloth and place it over the lower half of the pillow, leaving at least 50mm (2 inches) of pricking visible. Fasten the cloth with one pin at either side.

Working information

The person new to the craft will understand this paragraph more readily as problems arise when making the lace. It is advisable to read it now but refer back when the information becomes relevant.

(i) *Pins*
To put the pins into the card, hold the pair of bobbins to left of the hole in the left hand. Raise the heads of the bobbins, this will lift the threads and make the hole easily accessible. A left handed person should hold the bobbins to the right of the hole and put the pins in with the left hand. Always slope the centre pins back and the side pins outwards. Leave pins in the work for at least 75mm (3 inches), a better tension will result if the pins at the edges are left in position for the length of the pricking.

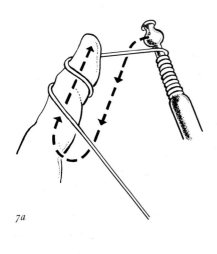

7a

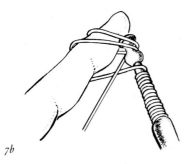

7b

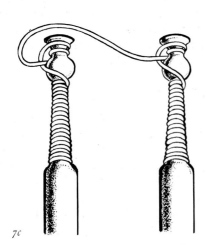

7c

(ii) *Threads*

The distance between pins and bobbins should not exceed 75mm (3 inches). To lengthen a thread, hold the bobbin in the right hand across the pillow and turn it towards the lace maker. To shorten a thread hold the bobbin in the left hand across the pillow, loosen the hitch with a pin and wind the bobbin towards the lace maker. This requires practice, but is important as thread becomes discoloured when handled. Knots are *never* worked into bobbin lace. When a knot appears, take another bobbin, fasten the thread on a pin behind the work and lay the new bobbin alongside the bobbin with knotted thread. Fasten them together with a wire twist or rubber band and work with a double thread for at least 25mm (1 inch), discard the old thread.

(iii) *Re-use of wound bobbins for the next pattern*

Patterns are always started using coupled bobbins; however, lace thread is expensive and should not be wasted. Take bobbins and tie together in pairs using reef knots, trim off ends of thread. Remove the hitches and wind the knot back onto one bobbin, replace the hitches and the pair is ready for use. The method of removing knots has been described in the previous paragraph. The lace in this book was made in this way and new threads introduced only when necessary.

(iv) *To move lace on the pillow*

This becomes necessary on the flat pillow. Cut pieces of thick felt, that are 50mm (2 inches) wide and 25mm, 50mm and 75mm (1, 2 and 3 inches) long. Place them to give a raised centre and slope at each end and sew together. Place the felt under the pattern so that the pins will be in the felt and not the pillow. With care the work may be moved up the pillow, to effect continuity a second pricking is made and placed below the first.

(v) *To correct errors*

The lace has to be undone. As stitches are untwisted, remove the pins as necessary. *Never* remove all the pins at once as the threads cannot be untangled.

3 Basic Stitches

The three basic stitches with some variations are shown in photograph 8. Each one is explained in the order in which it appears in the photograph. Using ten squares to 25mm (1 inch) graph paper (page 93, illus. 160c) make a pricking as shown in diagram 10. Prepare six pairs of bobbins wound with Fils a Dentelles. Set up the pillow and put pins in holes *A* to *F*. Hang one pair of bobbins around each pin and in some way mark the bobbins hanging from pin *F*. (A rubber band twisted around each is sufficient.)

1 Cloth stitch

Refer to illus. 9. Use pairs from *F* and *E*, and from left to right count the threads from *1* to *4*. The figures refer to the positions only and threads must be recounted before each move.

(a) Using one hand only lift *2* over *3*.

(b) Using both hands lift *2* over *1* and *4* over *3* at the same time.

(c) Using one hand only lift *2* over *3*.

The pairs have changed position and one cloth stitch is complete. Discard the right hand pair to the right of the pillow. Use the other pair and the pair from *D* to make a cloth stitch. Discard the right hand pair to the right of the pillow and work the next stitch with the other pair and the pair from *C*. Discard the right hand pair and work with the pair from *B*, and then the pair from *A*. The marked pair should be on the left hand side of the pillow; it has travelled from the right and is known as the weaver. Put a pin in hole *G* to the right of the weaver pair. Pass the right hand thread of the weaver pair over the left hand thread of the same pair. Repeat this movement which in future will be referred to as 'twist twice'. Twisting always takes place from right to left and cords the threads together around the pin. The weaver works back through the pairs hanging ready as follows. Work

cloth stitch with the weaver and the pair from *A*, discard the pair to the left of the pillow. Work the next cloth stitch with the weaver and the pair from *B*. Continue until the weaver is on the right hand side. Put pin *H* to the left of the weaver and twist the weaver pair twice. Note that the basic stitch movements are the same regardless of direction of travel of the weaver. Work back to *I*, then to *J* and continue until written instruction is unnecessary. The five pairs which hang straight down are known as passive pairs.

2 Cloth stitch and twist

Begin with the weaver at the right hand side and the pin in position. Refer to illus. 9 and using the weaver and adjacent pair work *abcb*. Continue across the work using cloth stitch and twist instead of cloth stitch. Note that the pairs hanging have one twist on them. This is part of the lace and should not be removed. In order to maintain good tension hold the weaver firmly at the end of each row and ease the passive pairs down. This stitch is used infrequently in this way. It is more often used as follows.

3 Cloth stitch with cloth stitch and twist edge

With the pin in position and the weaver on the right hand side work cloth stitch and twist with the first pair. Continue across the work through the next three pairs in cloth stitch. Twist the weaver once and work with the last pair in cloth stitch and twist. Twist the weaver once more and put up the pin to the right of the weaver as usual. Work cloth stitch and twist to cover the pin and continue through the next three pairs in cloth stitch. Remember to twist the weaver once before working cloth stitch and twist with the outside pair. Close scrutiny of the lace to clarify the

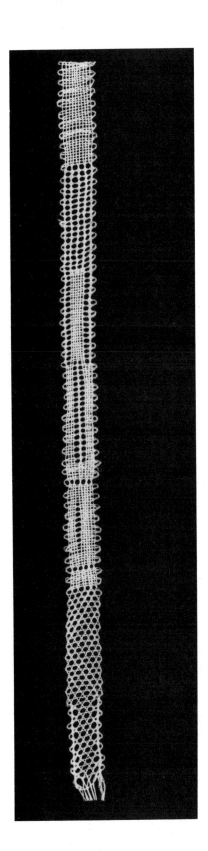

8

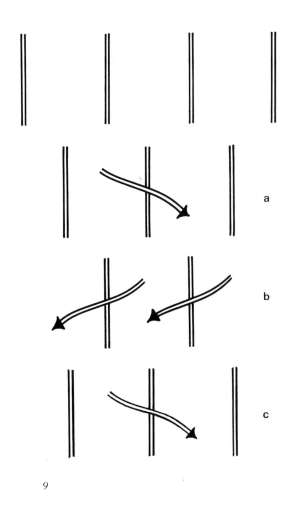

a

b

c

9

reason for adding the twist is worthwhile. When working away from the edge, the cloth stitch and twist stitch leaves a twist on the weaver and therefore a fine hole. On the other side the weaver is travelling from cloth stitch and it is necessary to add the twist to achieve the same effect.

4 Cloth stitch and twist in the centre of cloth

With the pin in position and the weaver on the right work cloth stitch through two pairs, twist the weaver once and work cloth stitch and twist with the next pair. Work cloth stitch through the remaining two pairs. Returning from left to right, work through two pairs in cloth stitch, twist the weaver once, work cloth stitch and twist with the centre pair, and complete the row in cloth stitch. As the cloth stitch and twist is in the centre of cloth it is necessary to give the weaver the twist when approaching from either direction.

5 Horizontal break in cloth stitch

This is achieved by twisting each passive pair once when the weaver is at the end of a row. Cloth stitch only is worked throughout.

6 Vertical break in cloth stitch

Using the weaver work through a set number of passive pairs in cloth stitch (in this case two pairs). Twist the weaver and continue to the end. On the return stop in the same place, twist the weaver and continue to the end. Continue making the break as long as required. To make the break assume an oval rather than a straight line work across, introducing the twists as before. Gradually increase the number of twists to a central point and reduce them to achieve a symmetric effect.

7 Half stitch

Remove any identification remaining on the bobbins. With the pin in position and the weaver on the right hand side use the weaver and adjacent pair to work a half stitch which, referring to illus. 9 is *ab*. Discard the right hand pair and work a half stitch with the next pair. Discard and continue to the end. It will be seen that one thread only travels across the lace and the passive threads hang twisted. At the end of the row the pin will be put in to the right of the last two threads. One twist is given before these work a half stitch to begin the return row.

8 Half stitch with a firm edge

With pin in position and weaver on the right hand side, work a cloth stitch and twist to cover the pin. Continue through the next four pairs in half stitch, then work cloth stitch and twist with the last pair. Put up the pin and give the weaver to the left of the pin one twist. Cover the pin with cloth stitch and twist and work as far as the last stitch in half stitch. This gives a firm edge that will withstand use and laundering.

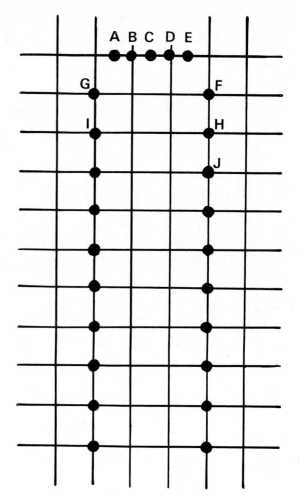

10

4 Tape Lace

Made with very few bobbins and worked in the same way as the strip of basic stitches in the previous chapter, tape lace offers an opportunity for the inexperienced person to practise in an interesting way. The simple edging described below should be worked as a preparation for the other lace in this chapter.

Simple edging

Refer to photograph 11 and prepare pricking 12 and as described on page 12. The ink lines should be marked in very carefully. The requirements are:

6 pairs bobbins wound with DMC Fils a Dentelles no. 70

Crochet hook

Piece of transparent rigid plastic 75 × 125mm (approx. 3 × 5 inches)

Place the pricking on the pillow with pins at the four corners only. Two cover cloths are used, one to cover the top edge of the pricking and the other to cover the lower part, leaving about 75mm (3 inches) exposed. Refer to working diagram 13 and put pins in holes A and B. Hang two pairs in order on A, so that the bobbins from the same pair lie adjacent to each other. Similarly hang three pairs on B. These are the passive pairs that will remain straight throughout the tape which is worked entirely in cloth stitch. Hang one pair on a pin at a, this will fall to the right of the other pairs and is the weaver. As the same weaver is used for the complete pattern, the bobbins may be marked for easy recognition, or a coloured thread used to add variety. To begin: Take the weaver on pin a and the next pair to the left (the right hand pair from A) and work cloth stitch. Discard the right hand pair and work a cloth stitch with the weaver and the next pair to the left. Continue until

five stitches have been worked and the weaver is on the left hand side. Twist the weaver twice and put up pin b to the right of the weaver pair. Work in cloth stitch with the weaver through the five pairs back to the right hand side. Twist the weaver twice and put up pin c to the left of the weaver pair. The black line on the pricking indicates the position of the weaver, continue until eight pins have been put into the lace. Now remove pins A and B and ease the passive threads down to achieve a neat beginning. To maintain good tension refer to the notes at the end of the instructions for this pattern. Continue to work the tape in cloth stitch, the beginning and working are exactly the same as for *basic stitch no. 1*, page 14.

Work e normally, giving two twists to the weaver as it travels around the pin. Ignore the other black line at this pin hole until later.

When pin f is in position work five cloth stitches to the right towards g.

As pin g is a long way from the tape give the weaver eight twists, put up pin g and continue.

Work from h with five cloth stitches through the tape, give the weaver eight twists, pass it round pin g and continue.

The use of plastic: As the tape curves around, it becomes difficult to work, since threads catch on pins. Press the pins down until the heads touch the card and put the piece of plastic over the pin heads. The cover cloth will hold it in place, but it is not usual to pin it in position as it is moved frequently.

Work pins s and t normally, ignore the other lines until later.

Weave from j through the five pairs to the right and twist the weaver four times. Remove pin g.

Pin g is used for the last time and the loops around the pin must be fastened together. Put a small hook through the long loops and hook one of the weaver threads up through both loops. Put the other weaver

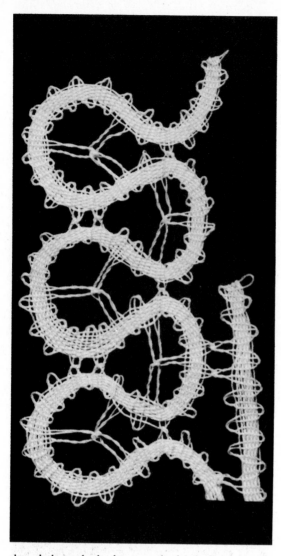

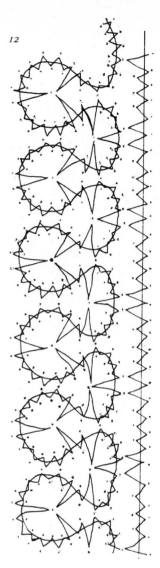

thread through the loop on the hook. Remove the hook and pull both weaver threads firmly. Tie one single knot to hold the threads together at the centre. Twist the weaver pair three times more and continue the tape. Put the pin back in the centre pin hole.

Work *k* to *m* as *f* to *g*.

Work *e* similarly to *g*. Cloth stitch is worked through the tape from *m*. Pin *e* is removed and a hook put through the hole to pick up one of the weaver threads. The other thread is passed through the loop and both are pulled firmly. A knot is tied to hold them in position. Pin *e* is replaced. Refer to page 70.

n to *m* are worked as *h* to *g*.

E to *m* are worked as *j* to *g*.

s and *t* are worked as *e*.

The straight tape on the right hand side is worked as described on page 14. A hook is used to link it to the rest of the lace. Alternatively both tapes are worked at the same time and linked as follows. Take the weaver from each tape and work them together in cloth stitch, put up the pin in between the pairs. Work another cloth stitch and the weavers continue in their own tape trail.

Possible faults and how to improve the result:

1 *Large ugly loops around pins showing when lace is removed from pillow*

(i) Insufficient twisting of the weaver around the pin.

(ii) Pulling the passive pairs too much. With prac-

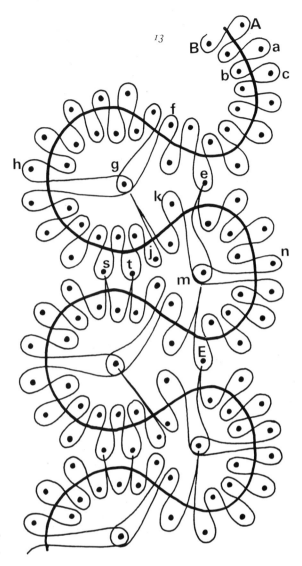

13

Motif no. 1

Photograph 14 and pricking 15 (the pricking is shown sideways for easy reference when making the lace) show a small piece of lace which can be mounted under a 70mm (2¾ inch) paperweight or may be used as a decoration, for example on the pocket of a blouse. You need six pairs of bobbins wound with DMC Fils a Dentelles no. 70.

Make a pricking and pin it in the centre of the pillow. Use four cover cloths to conceal the edges of the card.

Place a pin in the ringed hole and hang the weaver around it, it may be marked in some way to facilitate recognition. Hang three pairs on a pin in hole *a* so that the bobbins of the same pair lie adjacent to each other. Similarly hang two pairs on pin *b*. Weave to the left through five pairs, beginning with the pair on the ringed pin (weaver) and the right hand pair from *a*. When five cloth stitches have been made the

14

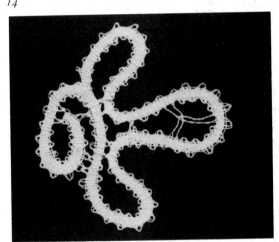

tice the lace maker learns to achieve good tension; on the inner edge of the curve the pairs are pulled very firmly but on the outer edge allowance must be made for the increased distance that the passive pairs travel. To keep the edge pairs close to the pins and prevent loops, the tensioning should be slight and the pairs encouraged to remain on the outer curve.

2 *Untidy joining of threads*

(i) Loss of twists on the weaver.

(ii) Insufficient twisting when the weaver travels an increased distance.

(iii) Omitting the twists after the join is made.

(iv) A hook which is too large and distorts the hole.

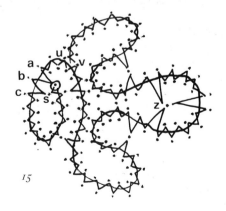

15

weaver should be on the left hand side. Put in pin *s* to the right of the weaver and twist the weaver twice. Work five cloth stitches back to the right. The black line on the pricking indicates the hole to use. Put up the pin to the left of the weaver pair, twist twice and weave back through the five passive pairs which make the tape. Continue, when eight pins are in position remove pins *a* and *b* and ease the threads down to achieve a neat beginning.

Pin *s* has been used already and this time it is necessary to make a join. A description of the method appears on page 70.

For the ringed hole, another join is made as at *s*.

Whenever a hole is used more than once a join is made on the last occasion that the weaver travels to the hole.

z is worked in the same way as *g* in the previous pattern on page 18.

A join is made at *u*, and the weaver travels back to *v*.

A join is made at *v* and a double knot is tied.

Allow 100mm (4 inches) thread to remain and cut off the bobbins. Remove all pins. Place the motif on the fabric on which it is to be mounted and, using a sewing needle, take the ends through to the wrong side of the fabric. Instructions for mounting lace are given in chapter 9.

16

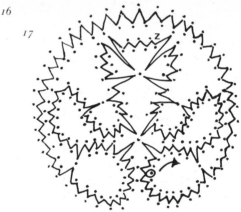

17

Motif no. 2

Photograph 16 and pricking 17 show a second motif suitable for a paperweight, alternatively it would look attractive mounted in a powder compact. Prepare the pricking and six pairs of bobbins wound with DMC Fils a Dentelles no. 70. Turn the pillow so that the motif appears upside down. The ringed hole is on the left hand side of a trail which makes a trefoil design (upside down) and then encircles it. Hang the weaver pair on a pin placed in the ringed hole. Place pins in holes to the back of the pillow to support the five passive pairs. As the pins are used temporarily and removed when the threads are pulled down for a neat beginning, the choice of pinholes is unimportant. Use the weaver to work to the right through five pairs in cloth stitch, twist the weaver twice and put up the pin as in the previous pattern. Continue to work the tape in cloth stitch, making sewings when appropriate. At *z* the weaver is twisted as described under *basic stitch no. 6*, page 16. When the trefoil part of the trail is complete, the form of the tape

changes at the outer edge where cloth stitch and twist is introduced. Refer to *basic stitch no. 3*, page 14. As the trail becomes wider, the weaver is twisted to fill the space, again refer to *basic stitch no.6*, page 16. The motif is completed according to the instructions for motif no. 1.

Motif no. 3

Photograph 18 and pricking 19 show a delicate piece of lace, no additional knowledge is required, but care is needed to work with fine thread and negotiate the curves of the longer, more complicated trail. It is essential to make an accurate pricking. Five pairs of bobbins wound with DMC Retors D'Alsace no. 50 are required.

To begin hang the weaver pair on a pin placed in the ringed hole. Hang four pairs behind on support

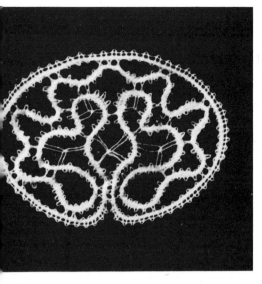

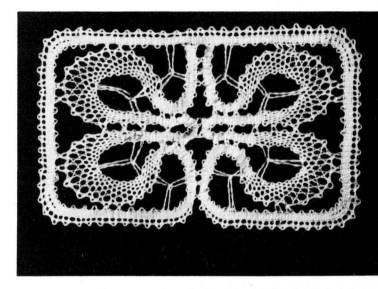

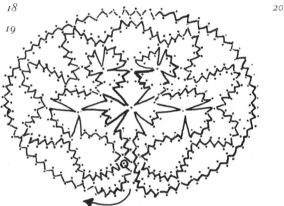

18

19

20

21

pins and weave to the right to begin the cloth tape with a cloth stitch and twist outer edge. The oval frame of tape is worked first and the sewings will be made only when the inner cloth tape is worked. Close study of photograph and pricking explain the method.

Motif no. 4

The lace in photograph 20 is a suitable size for an oblong paperweight. Prepare pricking 21 and six pairs of bobbins wound with DMC Fils a Dentelles no. 70. The ringed hole indicates the position of the weaver. The five passive pairs fall to the right of the weaver and half of the tape within the shape is worked before the framework. This pattern is more complicated in that the tape varies in width and half stitch is introduced to accommodate this. As the width

increases half stitch with cloth stitch and twist edges is worked in the same way as in *basic stitches nos. 7 and 8*, page 16. As the tape becomes narrow cloth stitch is used and it is important to pull the passive pairs firmly as the five pairs lie very close together. The weaver lines on the pricking indicate clearly the method of working the motif. It is finished in the same way as motif no. 1.

Spiral mat

The spiral mat, shown in photograph 22 and pricking 23 is worked from the centre out to the decorative edge using seven pairs of bobbins wound with DMC Pearl cotton no. 12. One cannot over-emphasize the need for clearly marked prickings, since the lines are the only guide and the success of the lace depends on them.

To begin, ascertain that the pricking on the pillow is in the same position as the copy in the book. Place pins in the holes on either side of *o* and hang three pairs of bobbins in order on each pin. These are the passive pairs. The weaver pair must lie to the right of these on a pin in the ringed hole. Weave to the left through the six passive pairs and put up a pin to the right of the weaver pair, twist the weaver twice. The line on the pricking indicates which hole is used. Work eight pins and then remove the support pins on either side of *o*. Ease the passive threads into position to achieve a flat and neat beginning. When the spiral trail reaches the ringed hole a sewing is

made, which is described on page 70. It is always more difficult to make a sewing through a single loop and care is needed to avoid breaking the thread. Continue the cloth stitch spiral, making sewings when necessary, until pin *t* is reached.

At *t*, study the photograph; cloth stitch and twist is introduced on both sides of the tape. Refer to *basic stitch no. 3*, page 14.

Ignore the letters at pins *y* and *z*; they are used later when the trail is complete.

From *u* the large curved trail is worked in half stitch with cloth stitch and twist edges. Refer to *basic stitch no. 8*, page 16. Care is required to get good

tension on the outside edge.

A sewing is made at the pin immediately before pin v. At v the trail changes to cloth stitch with the cloth stitch and twist edges until the next large curve from u.

To work a pattern of this type it is essential to study the photograph and to understand where and why different stitches are used. The complete edge is worked.

At y, make a sewing and weave back to z.

At z, make a sewing and finish it securely with a double knot.

Using the hook, pull one thread of each passive pair through pin holes between y and z or through the small spaces left by the cloth stitch and twist edge. Knot the threads of each pair together firmly.

Cut off the bobbins allowing 100mm (4 inches) of thread to remain on all except the outer left side thread which should be 250mm (10 inches) long. Remove all pins and remove the lace from the pillow. Lay the short threads along the edge of the cloth spiral and the long thread is used to oversew them in position. If the short threads are discarded gradually they will be unnoticed when the lace is turned over. It is usual to consider the underside of the lace to be the right side.

5 Adaptation and Use of Tape Lace

It is important to realize that simple tape lace is merely the first step towards confidence with pillow and bobbins and a true understanding of bobbin lace. Many people will use their skills to make traditional lace – Beds-Maltese, Bucks Point or Honiton. Others may wish to develop the basic techniques to produce original work. Regardless of this decision, it is essential to understand the reasons for every bobbin movement – nothing is gained by the person who learns to make one particular pattern but cannot apply the principles to the next. The learning process must include new techniques which can be applied to future work. Some of the knowledge acquired as one becomes adept at a variety of laces may be incorporated into tape lace patterns. The lace is versatile, it can be used for motifs, initials, braids and trims for dress or furnishings, edgings for table linen or it may be adapted to make designs for pictures. Some of the patterns in this section will rely on techniques explained later; page references are given but it may be easier to master the technique in context of a particular pattern and return to this section afterwards. A braid is enhanced by the addition of a raised gimp (photograph 24). Use pricking in diagram 10 prepared for the basic stitches. The requirements are:

7 pairs of bobbins wound with DMC Fils a Dentelles no. 70

2 pairs of bobbins wound with DMC Pearl cotton no. 5

Alternatively a pricking can be prepared on a graph with eight squares to 25mm (1 inch) and Pearl cotton no. 12 used for the tape and Twilley's Staylite used for the gimp threads. Set the pillow up to begin the tape as described on page 14 but with six pairs of passives instead of five. Weave across from right to left in cloth stitch, twist the weaver twice and put up the pin. Add one more support pin and hang on one

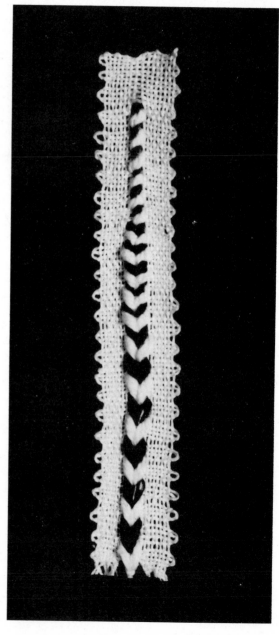

24

gimp pair to fall in the centre, with three passive pairs on either side.

To work the corded gimp
(The weaver is on the left.) Refer to illustration 25.

Work three cloth stitches to the centre.

Place the right hand gimp over the left.

Keep the weaver threads together and pass them over the first gimp and under the second. Work three cloth stitches to complete the row, twist the weaver twice and put up the pin.

Work three cloth stitches to the centre.

Place the right hand gimp over the left.

Keep the weaver threads together and pass them under the first gimp and over the second. Work three cloth stitches to complete the row, twist the weaver twice and put up the pin.

Repeat this sequence. Different colour gimp threads will create a two colour cord.

To work the chain gimp
(The weaver is on the left.) Refer to illustration 26 and hang in one additional gimp pair to the left of the corded pair.

Work three cloth stitches to the centre.

Take the outside gimp threads over their partners so that they lie side by side in the middle.

Keep the weaver threads together and pass them under the first gimp, over the centre gimps and under the fourth gimp. Work three cloth stitches to complete the row, twist the weaver twice and put up the pin.

Work three cloth stitches to the centre.

Again take the outside gimp threads into the centre.

Keep the weaver threads together and take them under the first gimp, over the centre gimps and under the fourth gimp. Work three cloth stitches to the end of the row, twist the weaver twice and put up the pin.

Repeat this sequence. There are many variations, both in the use of colour and the number of cords introduced. Success depends on a closely woven braid which emphasizes heavy threads on top.

To increase the size of the 'links' of the chain
Move the gimp threads only when travelling from the left side. As there are two rows of stitches between gimp crossings the chain will be longer.

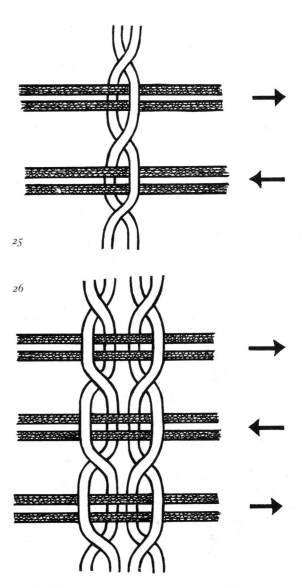

25

26

Tape lace edging with corner

Photograph 27 shows the lace with and without the raised chain gimp threads. To prick a length from pricking 28 work as follows. Rule a straight line on the pricking card, which will be the line on which all the right hand edge pins must lie. Prick the complete pattern, lift it and mark in the ink lines. Position the pattern to continue the pricking as a continuous length. The four ringed holes at the top of the pattern should lie over the four ringed holes at the end of the pricking. Ascertain that the right hand edge pin holes will fall on the ruled line. Prick the pattern. The ringed holes on the corner pattern will match those on the straight pricking.

To work over joins in the pricking

The card is never overlapped, it is cut so that the edges meet and there is continuity of pricking. To achieve this, place a straight edge across the pricking just below the last five ringed holes. Score a line across with a pricker. Bend the card to break the surface and cut off the excess card. On a pillow or pricking board, lay this pricking across the top of the next and match the pin holes. Scratch a line across the lower pricking, remove it from the pillow. The line should fall below the ringed holes, when the card is cut the ringed holes will appear on the top pricking only. The advantage of placing the prickings together and scratching the card is that one can be absolutely certain that the pricking will match before cutting.

Prepare six pairs of bobbins wound with pearl cotton no. 12 and one pair with a thicker yarn, e.g. Twilley's Staylite.

To begin

Hang the weaver on a pin on the right hand side of the trail. On support pins hang, from right to left, two pairs for the trail, one gimp pair and the three remaining trail pairs. In this pattern the gimp is not centrally placed as the extra pair on the left side will add interest around the large outer curve of the trail. Comparison of photograph with pricking will clarify the method. Sewings are made as described in the previous section and the cloth and twist feature on the left hand edge is worked as in *basic stitch no. 3*, page 14.

Crossing of trails

Refer to working diagram 29 which is an enlargement of the pricking. The trail is worked from *a* and *b* through *s*, *t*, *u* and *v* and on around the loop as indicated by the arrow. Weaving continues

27

26

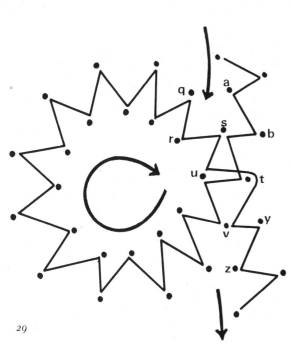

29

from *q* to *r* and on through *s*, *u*, *t* and *v* in that order. The trail travels over the trail worked previously and sewings are made at *s*, *u*, *t* and *v*. Many people will make two sewings only, at *u* and *t*.

The right hand edge
If desired a tape may be worked on the right hand edge – it improves the appearance when the lace is mounted.

To complete a square or rectangle
The trails must be joined firmly but neatly. Pin the beginning of the lace back onto the pricking and press the pin heads down. Use clear plastic to facilitate working, and complete the pattern using every pin hole available. Hook the weaver thread through the first pin used at the beginning, put the other thread through and knot them securely. The other pairs must be hooked through between the passive threads at the beginning and knotted firmly. Refer to instructions for cutting off bobbins and sewing off threads on page 70.

Motif with raised chain gimp

Photograph 30 shows the motif which is 75mm (3 inches) in diameter and has a variety of uses. There are several paperweights, trinket boxes and frames available to take lace of this size. In groups of three they make attractive mats and six groups of three will

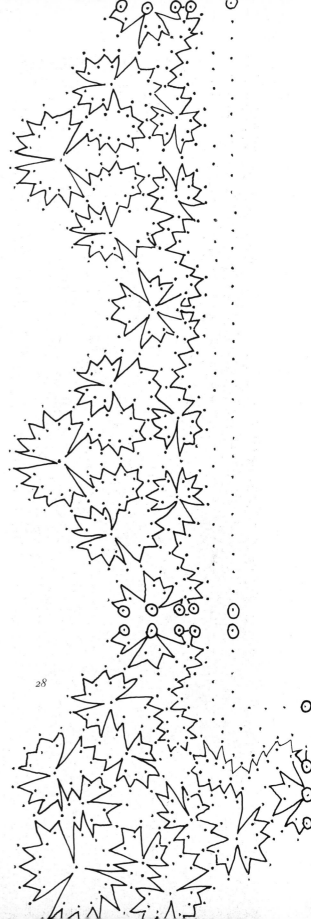

28

provide a decorative front for a 400mm (16 inch) cushion cover. This pricking is prepared by following 31. The extra hole below bottom centre is the centre point for groups of three. Seven pairs of bobbins wound with DMC Pearl cotton no. 12 and one pair wound with a thick yarn are required, the weaver is hung on a pin in the ringed hole, arrows indicate the direction of the trail. Work is completed at *y*. The threads are threaded through a mounting fabric as described on page 70 or knotted and sewn down, see page 71, according to the use of the lace.

As one understands the various stitches and techniques, experiment can take place to create motifs, pictures or wall hangings according to the needs of the individual. The remaining patterns in this section show three ideas. Study the photographs and prickings and try to associate parts of these patterns with others with which one is familiar. Note adaptations that have been made and try to decide why they are necessary. A simple design is preferable, not only for ease of working but also for its effect and impact. Guidance is given on the working of the swan, the boat and the balloon but success will depend on the ability of the lace maker to understand the use of threads as shown in the photograph and willingness to try out ideas to achieve the required result. For example, the number of pairs used to make the swan's body, or the number required for the half stitch fabric of the balloon is unimportant. Pairs are used to create the closeness of stitch for the effect needed in a particular situation.

The swan

Refer to photograph 32 and the pricking 33 and wind pairs with DMC Fils a Dentelles no. 70. Hang two pairs on pin *A* and make the first half of a leaf (refer to page 51). Hang two pairs on *B* and work similarly. These represent the beak. It is necessary to join in more pairs to work the head in cloth stitch. Put up pin *1* and place the pairs from the beak as follows. To the left of pin *1* put the left hand pair from *B*, the left hand pair from *A* and the right hand pair from *B*. Hang two pairs round pin *1*. Take the two threads to the left of pin *1* as weaver and twist them twice. Weave to the right through the other pair on pin *1* and through the right hand pair from *A*. Put up pin *2* to the left of the weaver and add one pair extra over the weaver as shown in diag. 34. Take this pair, place

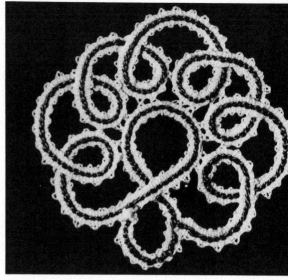

30

31

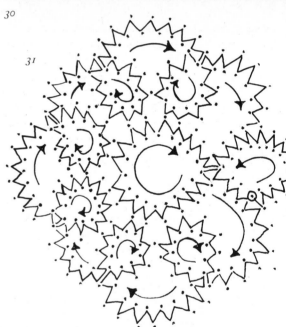

the thread under the weaver threads, and bring it up and behind the pin and allow it to lie inside one thread. If the weaver is kept firm a good tension is maintained. Weave through all pairs to the left and put up pin *3*, add one pair over the weaver. Work back to the right through all pairs, hang two more pairs side by side on a support pin behind the work and weave through these. Put up pin *4*. Added in this way the pairs give the characteristic bump on the swan's head. Add pairs as necessary to achieve close

32

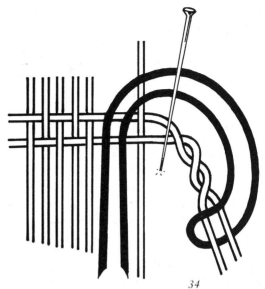

34

even cloth. The marking on the pricking and reference to diag. 35 clarify the working of the 'eye'. It will facilitate bobbin recognition to mark the original weaver when it is temporarily left as a passive pair. As the neck is worked, pairs on the outer curve should not be pulled too tightly, extra pairs are added as required. At *O* weave to the left through all pairs, but when travelling to the right, leave three or four pairs untouched each time. These will be reintroduced after *P* has been worked to correspond with the other side. Hook the weaver to the neck as shown and work the wing in half stitch. Half stitch is very suitable as it covers a wide area and is not distorted in less regular shapes. Hook the weaver to the cloth stitch as indicated. It is impossible to see the holes where half stitch crosses cloth. Either feel for the position with the pin or make holes as required. Finally work half stitch as tightly as possible. Do *not* discard pairs. Tie into a bundle as described on page 39. Leave long ends as these can be threaded to the back of the mounting material.

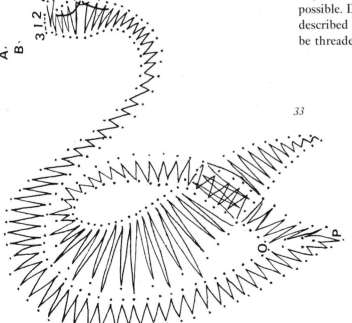

33

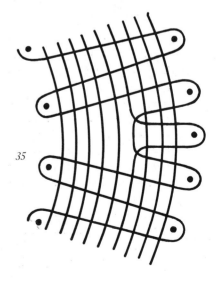

35

29

Boat

Refer to photograph 36 and pricking 37. DMC Fils a Dentelles is used. Begin with ten pairs round pin *A*. Refer to page 43. Introduce new pairs over the weaver at *m* and *n*, refer to page 29. From pin *n* make a twist in the centre of the cloth. At *B* weave in cloth stitch through six pairs to the centre and put up the pin to the right of the weaver. Using the pairs on either side of the pin make a cloth stitch. Both pairs are now weavers and continue separate trails. On the right hand side work the trail to *C* where an extra pair is added for the footside, which is described on page 48. To work the point at *D* refer to the instructions for the rear of the swan on page 29. The boat outline is completed at *E* and sewn into the trail. From *B* the left hand side trail is worked to *F* and pairs sewn into the trail. Three pairs are joined into the trail at *H* to work the inner cloth trail with two

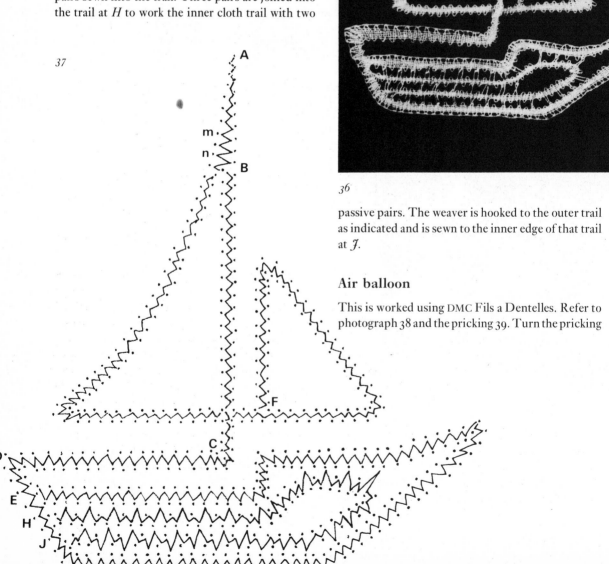

36

passive pairs. The weaver is hooked to the outer trail as indicated and is sewn to the inner edge of that trail at *J*.

Air balloon

This is worked using DMC Fils a Dentelles. Refer to photograph 38 and the pricking 39. Turn the pricking

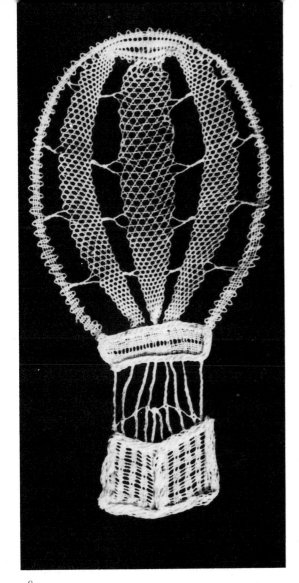

38

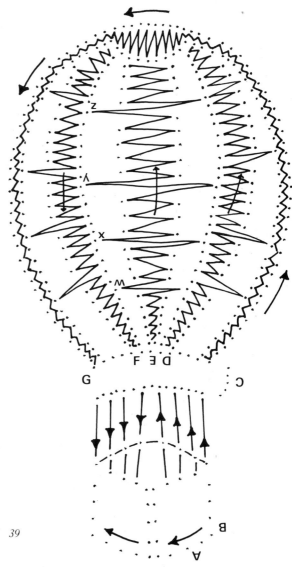

39

upside down and hang pairs on support pins at *A* and *B* to work half of the basket. Plaits are made to the collar and one pair twisted through to indicate the back of the basket. Pairs on support pins at *C* work through the plait pairs. Use can be made of the technique explained on page 88. Extra pairs are introduced at *D* and *E* and the cloth outline, the centre and one side panel are worked. To achieve an even effect the weaver from the centre panel is twisted out to pins at *w*, *x*, *y* and *z*. At the top of the balloon (the bottom of the pillow) the centre half stitch is ignored as the ends can be taken through mounting fabric later. The side half stitch pairs are incorporated into the cloth trail and the weaver is twisted to add interest. The pillow is turned, pairs

released for the half stitch panel, the weaver threads from the centre section are hooked in and the balloon completed to *F* and *G*. Some pairs are discarded at *F* and the collar worked to *G*. The pairs no longer needed are knotted together to maintain tension and the remaining threads are plaited back to the basket.

This idea uses the lace stitches to achieve a shape; as appearance is the first consideration it is unnecessary to fasten ends off, and they can be threaded out of sight to the back of the mounting fabric. However, the lace is easier to handle if adjacent threads are knotted together. The outline of the basket has been emphasised by a plait.

6 Torchon Lace

The making of Torchon lace is an excellent introduction to bobbin lace. The patterns move in a definite progression and, worked in order, should provide an understanding and logical approach to the craft.

Stitch practice

To make the lace one must be able to work the basic stitches described on pages 14–16 quickly, without reference to the stitch diagram. In addition it is necessary to understand the working of the straight edge, known as the footside; the braid in photograph 40 explains this. Prepare a pricking according to the graph pricking (41) on a graph with ten squares to 25mm (1 inch) and wind six pairs of bobbins with DMC Fils a Dentelles no. 70.

To begin the braid

Hang two pairs round pin *A*, so that the centre bobbins belong to the same pair. Similarly hang two pairs round pin *B*. On pin *Z* hang two pairs so that the bobbins of each pair hang side by side. Twist the bobbins to the right of pin *A* twice (i.e. put the right hand bobbin over the left and repeat so that there are two twists on these threads). Use the four threads at pin *A* and work cloth stitch and twist; this will enclose the pin. Twist the outer (right hand) pair once more and discard it to the right of the pillow. Use the other pair and the right hand pair from pin *Z* to make a cloth stitch and twist.

On the left hand side work in the same way. Twist the bobbins to the left of pin *B* twice. Remember that pairs are always twisted right over left. Use the four threads at pin *B* and work cloth stitch and twist to enclose the pin. Twist the left hand pair once more and discard to the left of the pillow. Take the other pair and the left hand pair on pin *Z* and work cloth stitch and twist.

To work the centre pin

Use the centre pairs to make a cloth stitch and twist. Put up pin *C* between the pairs. Work cloth stitch and twist to enclose the pin.

To work the footside on the right

Take the third pair from the right and travelling to the right, work cloth stitch and twist through two pairs. The pair is now on the outside edge. Put up pin *D* inside of the two pairs (i.e. to the left of four threads) and twist the outside pair once more. Ignore the outer pair and push it well to the right hand side. Use the other pair and the next to the left and work cloth stitch and twist. This will enclose pin *D*. This sequence is always worked on the Torchon footside.

To work the footside on the left

Take the third pair from the left and travelling to the left, work cloth stitch and twist through two pairs. The pair is now on the outside edge. Put up pin *E* inside of two pairs (i.e. to the right of four threads) and twist the outer pair once more. Ignore the outer pair and push it well to the left hand side of the pillow. Use the other pair and the next pair to the right to make cloth stitch to enclose the pin. Remove pin *Z*.

To work pin *F* follow instructions for working the centre pin. Continue to work the braid; *G* is worked as *D*, *H* is worked as *E* and so on. When this can be worked without reference to the text a tally can be introduced; this will not be required for the first patterns but is a pleasant addition to the braid.

The tally

In this case it is worked *instead* of a centre pin. Therefore use the centre pairs, each pair requires

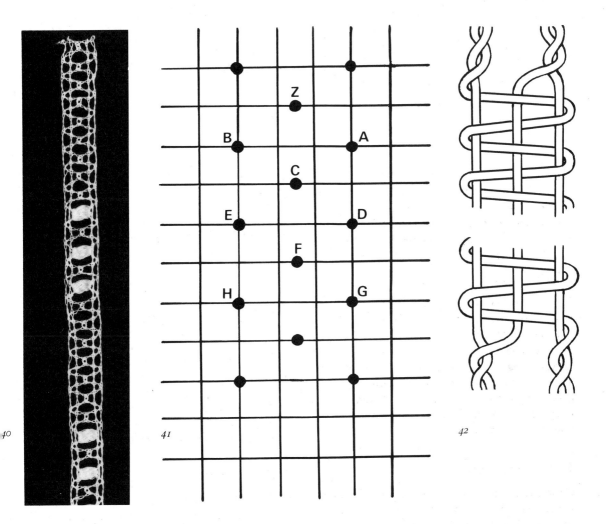

40 41 42

two twists. Refer to diag. 42. The shape of the tally is controlled by holding the outer threads taut and close to the twisted passive pairs. The weaver should be held in the hand throughout, as any weight or pull on the thread will destroy the tally shape. Take the left hand bobbin (as weaver) and pass it under the first, over the centre and under the right hand bobbin. It returns over, under and over. Refer to the illustration and continue to weave until the tally fills the space as in the photograph. Finish weaving with the weaver on the right and twist the threads on either side twice each. It is important to work the footside pin on the left. If the pin on the right is worked immediately, the tally weaver will be pulled and the shape of the tally lost. Tallies require much practice, the braid provides an excellent opportunity.

Terms used

Footside is the straight edge onto which the fabric is attached; on the pillow the footside is always on the right side for an edging, but of course is on both sides for an insertion.

Head (side) is the patterned decorative side of the edging. It is on the left hand side when the lace is being made.

Ground is the net or mesh and can be worked in a variety of ways.

Weaver is the pair of bobbins which travels across the cloth areas of the lace. Although only one thread actually travels across in half stitch, reference is made to the weaver pair which makes the stitch. The weaver lies in a horizontal position in the lace.

Passive threads hang down in cloth or half stitch or

33

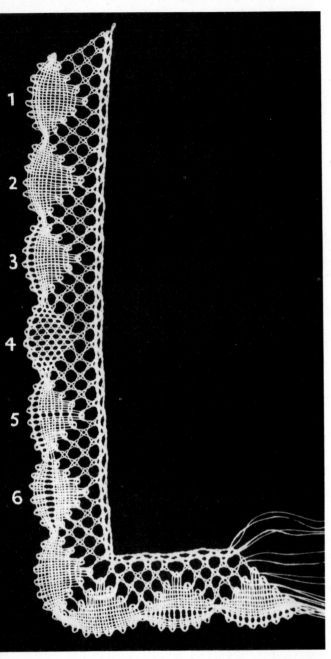

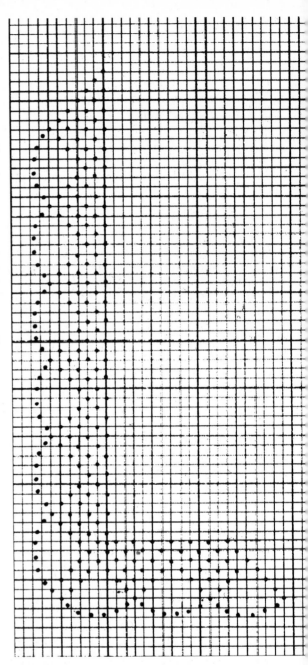

43   the pair which lies twisted parallel to the footside edge. In Torchon lace this pair may be pulled to reduce the length of the edging and gather the lace.

Direction of working

Weavers lie in a *horizontal* position, passive threads lie *vertically* but at other times all threads move diagonally. Pairs enter pattern features *diagonally* and leave *diagonally*. When in doubt as to the correct pairs to use at a particular pin, the lace maker will find that, if pairs are positioned to continue diagonal lines of travel, they will fall across the pin holes and stitches can be worked. The net ground is worked with pairs moving *diagonally* from pin to pin.

To prepare the Torchon pricking

Refer to general instructions on page 12. To make the pricking for the lace in photograph 43 refer to the dotted grid in pricking 44. Torchon lace is geometric and accurate prickings are made on graph paper, the size of the graph depending on the thread used. The following graphs/threads are recommended:

8 squares to 25mm (1 inch) DMC Pearl cotton no. 12

10 squares to 25mm (1 inch) DMC Fils a Dentelles no. 70

10 squares to 20mm ($\frac{3}{4}$ inch) DMC Retors D'Alsace no. 30

When the pattern has been transferred to graph paper it can be pricked onto card. One hole at either end of the footside is pricked and a pin put into each. A ruler is pushed against the pins and the row of footside holes can be pricked, the ruler ensuring a straight line. The remaining holes are pricked diagonally, using the ruler as a guide. Finally the headside curved line of holes is added. When the pricking is thought to be complete, lift the pattern and card with drawing pins. Hold it up to the light when any omissions are easily seen. Place it back onto the pricking board to add missing holes.

Note: The working diagrams in this section are on grids of ten squares to 25mm (1 inch) and can be traced for use with appropriate thread. However, better results will be obtained if the pricking is planned on graph paper. Refer to 44 and diagram 45. Ringed dots at either end of diagrams indicate holes which should be matched when making a length of pricking. Refer to page 25 for further explanation.

Torchon fan pattern

Refer to photograph 43 and diagram 45. Prepare eleven pairs of bobbins. Hang two pairs of bobbins on pin *A1* and one pair on each of pins *B, C, D, E* and *F*. Hang four pairs on pin *G*, side by side.

To begin

Twist the two right hand bobbins on *A1* twice, work cloth stitch and twist to enclose (cover) pin *A1*. Give one twist extra to the right hand pair and discard to the side of the pillow. Take the other pair and the pair from *B* to work cloth stitch and twist. Do *not* put up a pin. Discard the right hand pair. Take the other

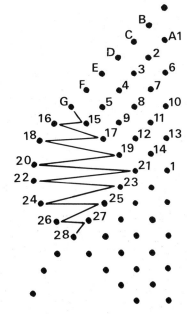

45

pair and the pair from *C* to make half stitch. Put up pin *2* between these pairs and work another half stitch with the same pairs to cover the pin. Discard the right hand pair. Take the other pair and the pair from *D* to make half stitch, put up pin *3* between these pairs and cover with half stitch. Discard the right hand pair. Continue, using the pair from *E* for pin *4* and the pair from *F* for pin *5*. Remove support pins *B, C, D, E* and *F*.

Footside and ground

The usual sequence is to work the footside pin and the diagonal row of ground at the same time. Take the third pair from the outside (right side) edge and work to the right with cloth stitch and twist through two pairs as described for the braid on page 32. Put up pin *6* inside (to the left of) two pairs. Give the outer pair an extra twist and ignore it. Take the other pair and the pair to the left of it (the passive pair) and work cloth stitch and twist to cover pin *6*. Discard this passive pair. The footside sequence is complete. Take the other pair (third from the edge) and the pair from pin *3* to work half stitch, put up pin *7* between the pairs and cover with half stitch.

Discard the right hand pair and use the pair from pin *4* to work half stitch, put up pin *8* and cover with half stitch. Discard the right hand pair and use the pair from pin *5* to work half stitch, put up pin *9* and cover with half stitch. Work the footside and ground sequence from *10* to *12* and *13* and *14*. Remember that pins *10* and *13* are worked with the third pair from the edge. The triangle of ground is complete and pairs hang diagonally for the fan, one pair to enter at each pin.

To work the fan

Begin at *G*, using the left hand pair as weaver. Work in cloth stitch to the right through the three pairs hanging on *G*. Work on to the right through one pair more that is hanging from pin *5*. Put up pin *15* between the pairs of the last stitch and twist the weaver (the pair to the right of the pin) twice. Use the weaver to work to the left through all pairs (four cloth stitches). Twist the weaver twice and put up pin *16* to the right of it. Weave back to the right through the four passive pairs and on through the pair hanging from *9*. Put up pin *17* between the pairs of the last stitch worked. Note that the pin is put into position to hold the weaver before it returns to the other side of the fan. Remember to twist the weaver every time it passes around a pin, work back to pin *18*. Continue to pin *22*, bringing extra pairs at pins *19* and *21*. From pin *22* work back to the right through all the passive fan pairs except one (i.e. through six pairs). Twist the weaver pair twice, put up pin *23* and work back to pin *24*. Notice that the pair brought in for pin *21* has been left out after that pin. From pin *24* work back to pin *25* through one passive pair less than the previous row (i.e. through five pairs). Work to pin *26* and back to pin *27* through one pair less (i.e. through four pairs). Work back to pin *28* but do not cover it. It is easier to find the weaver if it is at the extreme left of the work. Twist pairs hanging from pins *21*, *23*, *25* and *27* once each. One pattern repeat is complete.

Return to the ground. Work pin *1* as a normal footside pin and continue, remembering to work diagonally but not to work the last pin hole in each row as it will be needed for the fan.

Variations

See photograph 43.

1 and **2** cloth stitch.

3 cloth stitch and twist on the edge, refer to page 14.

4 half stitch with cloth stitch and twist on the outside edge only, refer to *basic stitch no. 8*, page 16.

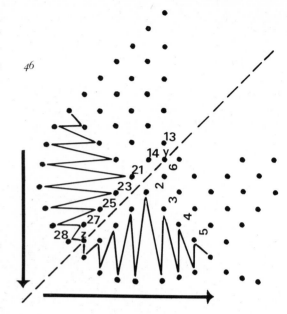

46

5 Twisted passive pairs after pin *21* is in position. Refer to *basic stitch no. 6*, page 16.

6 Twisted weaver in cloth. Refer to *basic stitch no. 5*, page 16.

To work the corner

Refer to the working diagram (fig. 46). Complete the pattern to corner line, indicated by the broken line. Pin *Y* is the corner footside pin, and is worked normally using the third pair from the edge (from pin *14*). Pin *Z* is the corner pin to link the fans. Take the fan weaver at pin *28* and weave to the right through three fan pairs, put up pin *Z* and weave back to the outside edge which will be the beginning of the next fan. Turn the pillow and work the fan. Study the ground carefully as the footside pin *Y* in the corner has been worked. The pair from the bottom of the fan and the pair from *Y* will work pin *2*. Work the row, pins *3*, *4* and *5*. The next row begins with footside pin *6*.

Circular fan edging

Shown in photograph 47 with the pricking 48, the pattern requires twelve pairs of bobbins wound with DMC Fils a Dentelles no. 70. The fan is larger than the fan in the previous pattern, but is worked in the same way with pairs entering and leaving after each pin. Begin at *A1*.

A1

47 (insert) 48

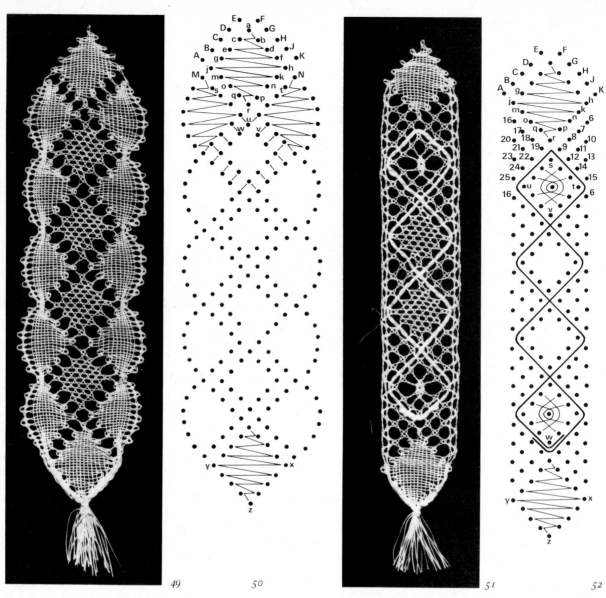

49 50 51 52

Fan and diamond sampler

Photograph 49 and working diagram 50. Prepare
sixteen pairs of bobbins. Hang one pair on *A–K*
inclusive.

To work the cloth diamond
Work cloth stitch with pairs from *E* and *F*. Put up
pin *a*. As the weaver travels to the right, the pair to
the left of pin *a* is the weaver pair. Twist it twice and
work two cloth stitches to the right, through the
other pair at *a* and through the pair on *G*. Twist the

weaver twice and put up pin *b* to the left of the
weaver. Remove pin *F* and ease the weaver into
position. Work to the left with cloth stitch through
the two passive pairs and the pair on *D*. Twist the
weaver and put up pin *c* to the right of the weaver.
Work back through three passive pairs and the pair
on *H*, twist the weaver twice and put up pin *d*.
Continue, working through one pair extra at each
pin to pin *j*. Remove the support pins. From pin *j*
work through eight passive pairs to pin *k*. The pair
from *K* that entered the diamond at *h* is not
included. Continue, working through one pair less

each time until two pairs remain at *r*. Remember to cover pin *r* with cloth stitch. Ten pairs hang from the diamond, twist each pair once.

To work the fan on the left side

Hang three pairs side by side on pin *M*. Bring the pair from *j* to fall to the left of these pairs, all other pairs fall to the right. The pair from *j* is the weaver, it works cloth stitch and twist with the left hand pair on *M* and on through the other two pairs with cloth stitch. Cloth stitch is also worked through the pair from *m* and pin *s* is put up to the left of the weaver. The fan is worked as the fan on the edging earlier in this section.

To work the fan on the right side

Hang three pairs side by side on pin *N*. Bring the pair from pin *h* to fall to the right of the pairs on *N*. The pair from *h* is weaver and works cloth stitch and twist with the right hand pair from *N*. It continues through three more pairs and pin *t* is put up. The weaver is to the left of the pin, it is twisted twice and weaves back to the outside edge with three cloth stitches, a twist on the weaver and cloth and twist on the edge pair. Continue.

The half stitch diamond

Check that one pair comes diagonally from each fan pin to make the diamond. These pairs should be twisted twice before entering half stitch. The pairs from the points of the fans make a half stitch, pin *u* is put up, the pair to the left of pin *u* is the weaver. It weaves through two pairs to the right and pin *v* is put up. Note that a pair has entered the diamond diagonally from the fan. Check that there are two weaver threads to the right of pin *v*. Weave back through three pairs to pin *w*. Continue and complete the diamond. Continue, working cloth fans and half stitch diamonds. Work the fans on both sides, and the last diamond in cloth stitch. Take in the weavers from the fans at points *x* and *y*. There should be two pairs only at pin *z*.

To complete the sampler

Take the pair from *x* through three pairs to the right in half stitch. Take the next pair hanging from the diamond out to the right through four pairs in half stitch; continue in this way until the pair from *z* works through seven pairs in half stitch and lies on the extreme right hand side. Take the pair from *y* to the left in half stitch and continue until the other pair from *z* is on the extreme left hand side. The outside pairs are used to bundle the threads together. Take the outer pair from each side and knot them together tightly. Cross them under the bundle, bring them round the threads and tie another knot. Allow 25mm (1 inch) to remain for a tassel, cut the ends off neatly.

Insertion sampler

Photo. 51 illustrates the sampler with gimp thread used to outline the pattern features. Spiders and half stitch diamonds are included. Twelve pairs of bobbins are required, and one pair extra wound with a thicker gimp thread. Gimp thread should be soft to lie flat and thick enough to be seen easily. Twilley's Lyscordet or Staylite is suitable for use with Pearl cotton no. 12. Pearl cotton no. 5 is suitable for most threads used in Torchon lace unless the work is very fine, when Pearl cotton no. 8 or no. 12 can be used.

To begin

Refer to the working diagram (fig. 52). Hang one pair of bobbins on pins *B* to *J* and two pairs side by side on pins *A* and *K*. Work the cloth diamond according to instructions in the previous pattern as far as *g*. Work in cloth stitch to the right through seven passive pairs in the diamond and through two pairs from *K*. Put up pin *h* and work through nine passive pairs and two pairs on *A* to put up pin *j*. The two pairs brought in for *h* are left out after *h*, therefore work through nine pairs only to *k* and seven pairs to *m*. Complete the diamond ending with two pairs at pin *r*. Remember to remove the support pins.

Footside and ground on the right

If necessary refer back to the instructions on page 35. The numbers given in the fan pattern will apply to this working diagram. The pair from *k* is the third pair to travel out to the footside. The pair from *n* works pin *7*, *p* works pin *8*, and *r* works pin *9*. Pin *15* is a footside pin worked with the third pair from the right, this comes from pin *14*. Remember to cover pin *15*.

Footside and ground on the left

This is similar to the working for the right hand side

but the footside is worked out to the left, as described for the braid on page 32 and the ground is worked to the right. Work as follows. Take the third pair from the left (the pair from *m*) out to the left through two pairs with cloth stitch and twist. Put up pin *16* to the right of two pairs, twist the outer pair once more and discard to the left side of the pillow. Cover the pin with the next two pairs. Discard the left hand pair and use the other pair and the pair from pin *o* to work half stitch, pin *17*, half stitch. The right hand pair and the pair from pin *q* work half stitch, pin *18*, half stitch. Return to the third pair from the edge and work out to the footside and pin *20*. Complete the ground on the left. Hang the gimp pair temporarily on pin *r* and allow it to fall centrally between pairs from *19* and *9*.

The use of gimp threads

These surround and emphasize parts of the pattern, pairs on either side of gimp threads must have two twists. Give one twist more to pairs from pins *25, 24, 22, 19, 9, 12, 14* and *15* and pass the gimp between the threads as follows. Take the right hand gimp thread and pass it to the right under the first and over the second thread of each pair. Take the left hand gimp thread and pass it to the left over the first and under the second thread of each pair. Twist the pairs twice to enclose the gimp thread.

To work the half stitch edge of the diamond

Hold the pairs from pins *9* and *19* and they will lie over pin *s*. Work half stitch, pin *s*, half stitch. The right hand pair from *s* and the pair from pin *12* work half stitch, pin, half stitch. Continue to pin *t*. On the other side the left hand pair from *s* and the pair from pin *22* work half stitch, pin, half stitch. Continue to pin *u*. To work the spider refer to diagrams 52 and 53. No pairs hang from *s* as they travelled diagonally working half stitch. One pair hangs from each of the two pin holes on either side. Ignore pairs from *u* and *t* (to be used later to work to *v* and for pins *6* and *16*).

The spider

Work with the centre four pairs only and twist each pair once more (three twists altogether). Take the centre left pair through two pairs to the right in cloth stitch. Take the left hand pair through two pairs to the right. The pairs have passed to the opposite side. Put up the centre pin allowing two pairs to fall on

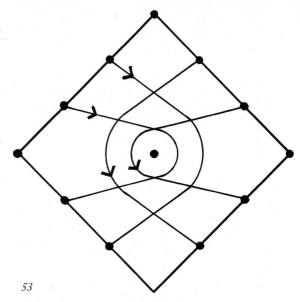

53

either side. Repeat the same bobbin moves as before, i.e. take the left centre pair through two pairs to the right and then the left pair through two pairs only in cloth stitch. (It is a common error to take the left hand pair through three pairs and then the spider will not lie flat.) Twist each pair three times.

To complete the half stitch edge of the diamond

Take the right side pair from the spider and the left hand pair from pin *t* and work half stitch, pin, half stitch. Take the next pair from the spider and the left hand pair from the last pin and work half stitch, pin, half stitch. On the other side take the right hand pair from pin *u* and the left hand pair from the spider and work half stitch, pin, half stitch. Use the last pair from the spider to complete the next pin. The centre pairs will meet diagonally to work pin *v*. The diamond and spider are complete.

Crossing gimp threads

The right hand gimp thread travels to the left (over and under) through the pairs from *t* to *v*. The left hand gimp travels to the right (under and over) through pairs from *u* to *v*. Pass the right hand gimp over the left.

Work the footside and ground on both sides. Take the gimp threads through four on either side for the half stitch diamond. For practice, spiders can be worked inside each diamond, a centre pin hole is necessary.

To complete the use of gimp thread

Work to pin *w* and bring the gimp threads to cross below that pin. Take the gimp threads on through two pairs as shown in the diagram. Lay the threads and bobbins back across the lace to help maintain tension; they can be cut off later. Twist all pairs as usual. There are no twists between the gimp threads.

To complete the sampler

Work the cloth diamond as described for the previous pattern, but bring in two pairs at pins *y* and *x*. Leave out two pairs after those pins. Complete with tassel.

Tally or spider patterns with half stitch edge

The lace in photograph 54 requires twelve pairs of bobbins wound with Fils a Dentelles, also one gimp bobbin wound with Pearl cotton no. 5. Prepare the pricking and refer to the working diagram (55).

Footside and ground

Work from *A1* as described previously; if necessary refer to the fan pattern, work to footside pin *6* and ground pin *7*. Use pairs from pins *4* and *7*, give one twist extra and work a tally as described on page 33. Leave the tally weaver on the right hand side supported to keep the shape of the tally. Work ground pin *9*. Work footside pin *10*, and very carefully use the tally weaver at pin *11*. Complete the ground so that four pairs are ready to enter the half stitch trail from pins *5, 9, 12* and *14*.

The gimp thread

Hang the gimp thread on *D*, twist the pairs from *5, 9, 12* and *14* once more and pass the gimp thread between them (under and over). Twist the pairs twice to enclose the gimp.

Half stitch trail

Hang one pair on *B* and the other four pairs on *C*. Use the weaver from *B* and the left hand pair from *C* to work cloth stitch and twist. Work half stitch through the other three pairs from *C* and the pair from pin *5*. Put up pin *b*, twist the weaver and work back to the outside edge, work cloth stitch and twist with the edge pair. Work from pin *c* with cloth stitch and twist and five half stitches which includes the

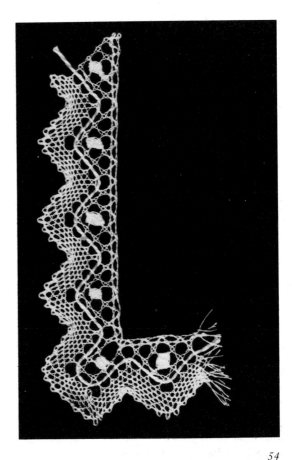

54

55

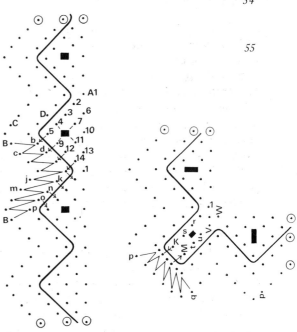

pair from pin *9*. Put up pin *d* and work back to the edge. Always work cloth stitch and twist before and after the edge pin. Continue, pairs are brought in from *12* and *14*, work to *j*. Work to *k* with cloth stitch and twist and six half stitches, put up the pin and return to the edge, put up pin *m*. The pair brought in from *14* at the point was left out after the point and not included at *k*. Work back to *n* with cloth stitch and twist and five half stitches; from the outside edge cloth stitch and twist and four half stitches are worked to *o*, and from the edge to *p* cloth stitch and twist and three half stitches are required. Stop at *B*. The trail is worked from *B* to *B* at one time, never stop in the middle. Pairs from the trail are ready for the ground and footside to be worked from *1*.

The corner
Work the straight edging as far as possible, i.e. the trail to *p* and the ground from *1* to *K*. Use the usual sequence (the third pair from the edge) to work the corner pin and remember to cover it. Work the trail from *p* to *q*, taking in one pair from *K* and leaving out one pair for *M*. The gimp is taken through as necessary, turn the pillow. A tally cannot be worked instead of a ground stitch but may be worked between the stitches. Use pairs from *r* and *s*, and when complete leave the tally weaver on the right. The pair from *K* and the pair from the trail work half stitch, pin *M*, half stitch. The right hand pair from *M* and the left hand pair from the tally make a half stitch, pin *t*, half stitch. The right hand pair from *t* and the right hand pair from the tally work half stitch, pin *u*, half stitch. The right hand pair from *u* and the weaver from the corner pin work half stitch, pin *V*, half stitch. Work the trail and then the footside and ground from *W*.

The spider pattern may be pricked from diag. 55, but three pins are omitted and one central spider pin hole made. Refer to photograph 56 and diagram 57.

To begin
Work *A1* and *2*, footside and ground stitches.

Half stitch trail
Hang one weaver pair on *B*, four pairs side by side on *C* and three pairs side by side on *D*. Work the trail as for the previous pattern. Four pairs enter the trail, three from pin *D* and one from pin *2*. Remove pins *C* and *D*. Work to *p*.

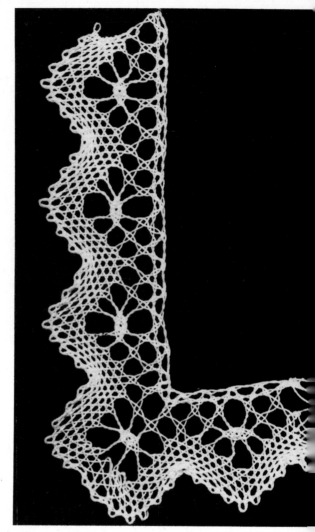

56

57

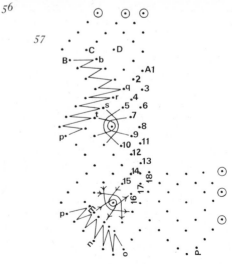

Footside and ground

Work pins *3*, *4* and *5* using pairs from *q* and *r* for stitches at *4* and *5*. Work pins *6* and *7*.

Spider

Pairs from *t*, *s*, *5* and *7* make the spider. Twist the pairs three times and work the spider as described on page 40. Twist the legs three times.

Footside and ground

Work pins *8*, *9*, *10*, *11*, and *12*. This provides pairs for the trail, work from *p* to *p*.

The corner

Work footside and ground pins *13*, *14* and *15* and the corner pin. Note that the spider pairs come from different positions because of the limitation of the corner. The trail continues to *n* and one pair is left out after *m*. Turn the pillow diagonally and use pairs as shown to make the spider. Continue the trail, bringing in the left hand spider leg as indicated in the diagram. Work to *o* and turn the pillow. The right hand spider leg and the pair from *15* work half stitch, pin *16*, half stitch. Pairs from *14* and *16* work *17*. Work the trail to *P*. Pairs enter from the spider and from pins *16* and *17*. Work ground pin *18* as pin *3* and continue.

The spider and rose ground sampler

Refer to photograph 58 and working diagram 59 and prepare sixteen pairs of bobbins wound with Fils a Dentelles. Hang all pairs round pin *A*, one pair inside the next so that the extreme outside threads will belong to the same pair. The centre bobbins are the only two of a pair that lie side by side. Twist the right hand threads twice and work cloth stitch and twist with the next pair. Continue to the left through all the pairs in half stitch, the last pair is worked with cloth stitch and twist. Put up pin *B*, cover with cloth stitch and twist and work back in half stitch to *C*. Cloth stitch and twist is worked both sides of the outer pins for a firm edge. Continue until pin *G* is in position, work back through eight pairs and put up the centre pin to the right of the weaver, cover with half stitch. Both pairs become weavers and weaving continues to position *P* on both sides. Leave out pairs on the inner edge of the trail as in the previous pattern for the cloth

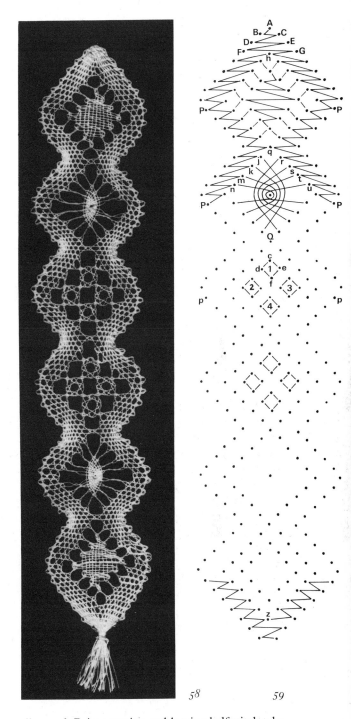

58   59

diamond. Pairs entering and leaving half stitch take one twist extra. Work the cloth diamond.

Trail

Work both trails to *q*, bringing in four pairs on each side from the cloth diamond. The weavers work half stitch, pin *q*, half stitch, and continue to weave to *P*. Four pairs will be left out on each side for the spider.

Spider

Regardless of size, the principle for working spiders is the same. Give each pair three twists. Take the left centre pair (from *j*) to right through four pairs. The pair from *k* works in cloth stitch through the same four pairs. Pairs from *m* and *n* work through the same four pairs. Put the pin in the centre. Repeat the bobbin movements, i.e. the left centre pair works to the right through four pairs and the others in order work through the same four pairs. Twist the pairs three times and work the trails to *p*, remembering to join them at pin *Q*.

Rose ground

This is always worked as a unit of four pins, work units in number order and for method refer to fig. 60. Two pairs enter diagonally each side of each unit. Isolate the four pairs and work as follows: two left

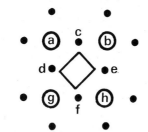

60

side pairs work cloth stitch and twist at *a* (no pin is used), two right side pairs work cloth stitch and twist at *b* (no pin is used). Centre pairs work half stitch, pin *c*, half stitch. Left side pairs work half stitch, pin *d*, half stitch. Right side pairs work half stitch, pin *e*, half stitch. Centre pairs work half stitch, pin *f*, half stitch. Left side pairs work cloth stitch and twist at *g* (no pin is used). Right side pairs work cloth stitch and twist at *h* (no pin is used). In the diagram the rings round letters indicate that no pins are used when those stitches are worked. Also when working several rose ground units, if the stitch indicated by the letter has been worked at the completion of one unit it is not worked again for the next.

To complete the sampler

Work the trail as indicated in the diagram. At *Z* the

61

weavers work together with half stitch, pin *Z*, half stitch. One weaver continues and the other becomes a passive pair in the half stitch. At the bottom use the outside pairs to tie the threads together as described on page 39.

The spider and diamond pattern

The half stitch trail is used again as the headside decoration in this pattern in photograph 61. Refer to the working diagram 62 to make the pricking and prepare seventeen pairs of bobbins wound with Fils a Dentelles.

Hang two pairs on *A1*, one pair on *B* and four pairs on *C*.

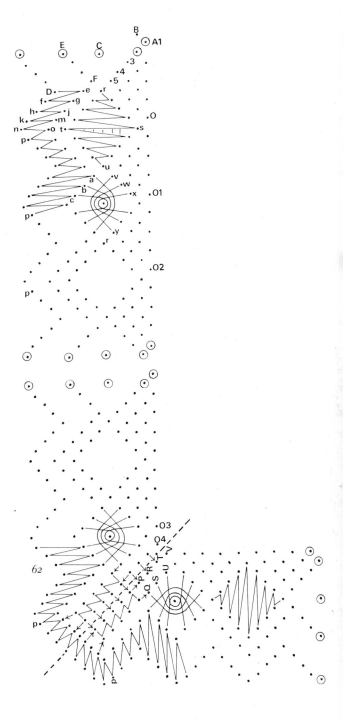

The footside and ground

Work to pin O on the footside. If necessary refer to the instructions for the fan pattern on page 35. Remove support pins C and B.

The half stitch trail

Hang one pair on D and eight pairs on E, side by side. Using the pair on D as weaver work cloth stitch and twist with the left pair on E. Continue to weave to the right through the other seven pairs in half stitch. Twist the weaver and put up pin e to the left of the weaver pair. Weave back through seven pairs in half stitch, work cloth stitch and twist with the outside pair. Twist the weaver (outer) pair once more and put up pin f to the right of the weaver. Work cloth stitch and twist to cover the pin and then six half stitches. Twist the weaver and put up pin g to the left of the weaver. Weave back to the left through six half stitches and work cloth stitch and twist on the edge. Put up pin h. From h to j one cloth stitch and twist and five half stitches are worked, from k to m one cloth stitch and twist and four half stitches, and from n to o one cloth stitch and twist and three half stitches. Leave the weaver on the extreme left at pin p. Check that one pair hangs from each of pins e, g, j and m.

The cloth stitch diamond

The last diagonal row of ground from pin 5 to pin O allows five pairs to hang ready for use on the diamond. Four pairs hang from the half stitch trail. Hang one pair from pin F to fall to the right of the pair from e. This provides for five pairs for the left side of the diamond. Begin with a cloth stitch using pairs from F and pin 5. Put up pin r and continue to work the cloth diamond. At pin s the pair taken in comes from the footside. There are two pairs remaining on the right not included. After pin t is in position the passive pairs receive one twist each to make the break in the cloth stitch. Refer to *basic stitch no. 5*, page 16. Complete the diamond covering pin u with cloth stitch, twist all pairs for ground or trail.

Footside and ground

Work three rows of ground to provide pairs for the spider. The last pins worked in each row are v, w and x.

The half stitch trail

The weaver lies to the left of pin p, work across through the four passive pairs (one cloth stitch and twist and three half stitches) and on through one pair more from t. Put up the pin and work back to the outside edge. Each time the weaver travels to the right it includes one pair extra from the diamond. Pairs are left out after *a*, *b* and *c*. Always work the trail from *p* to *p* without stopping.

The spider

Refer back to diag. 62. There are three pairs available on each side, from *c*, *b* and *a* and from *v*, *w* and *x*. Twist each pair three times. Work in cloth stitch, taking the pair from *a* through three pairs to the right. Take the pair from *b* through three pairs, and the pair from *c* through three pairs. The pairs remain in the same order. Put up the centre pin. Repeat the order of working by taking the left centre pair through three pairs to the right and then the other pairs follow in order. Twist the pairs three times. Three pairs move diagonally to the right into ground and three to the left into the trail.

Footside and ground

Take the third pair from the right hand edge and work out to the footside at *O1*. Using the spider pairs work ground stitches including pin *y*. Continue to *O2*. Remember to leave a diagonal row of holes from *r* for the diamond.

The half stitch trail

The weaver lies to the left of pin *p*. Work the trail taking in one spider pair at each pin. The last pair is taken in at the point of the trail, it will be left out after the pin for *r*. Always work the trail to pin *p*.

The corner

Work the spider. Work two rows of ground from the footside pins *O3* and *O4*. Work the corner pin. Work the half stitch trail to pin *p*. Instead of one diamond two narrow strips of cloth are made, one on either side of the corner diagonal. Work the cloth according to the diagram. Work the trail to *P*, taking in and leaving out pairs as shown. Turn the pillow and work the second cloth strip.

The ground

As the pillow has been turned it is necessary to complete rows of ground. Arrows indicate the pairs for pin *P*. The left hand pair from *P* and the pair from the corner of the cloth work pin *Q*. Work *R* and *S*, *T* and *U*. Pin *V* will be worked later, when the trail and spider have been completed.

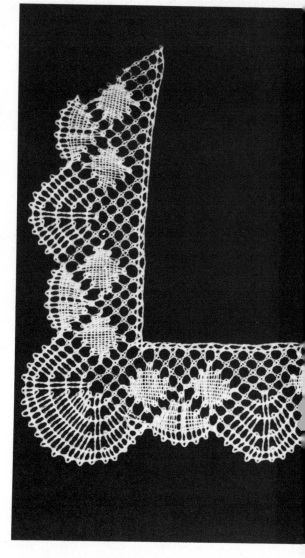

The Torchon fan pattern

This fan is worked in cloth stitch and twist and is peculiar to Torchon lace. Refer to photograph 63 and diagram 64. Torchon lace can be made quite quickly provided that one adheres to a strict order of work. This is explained by reference to this pattern. Set in the footside and ground and work rows from *X* to *Y* to provide pairs for the cloth diamond.

Order of work

(i) Work the cloth diamond.

(ii) Work the cloth fan. To begin hang three pairs on *A*, weaver and two passive pairs. The edge of the

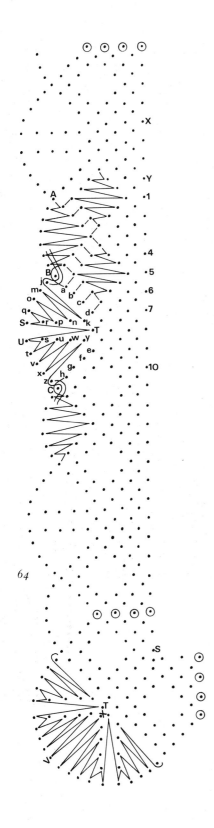

fan is worked with cloth stitch and twist.

(iii) Work footside and ground rows *1* to *4*.

(iv) Work the next cloth diamond.

(v) Work the row of ground stitches *a* to *d*. Use the weaver from the fan and the pair from the point of the diamond for half stitch, pin *a*, half stitch. Use the right side pair from *a* and the next pair from the diamond for *b* and so on.

(vi) Work the ground from pin *5*.

(vii) Work the cloth stitch and twist fan described below.

(viii) Work a long row of ground from *6* to *h*.

These eight points make the pattern. Repeat the points in this order.

The cloth stitch and twist fan

Use the pairs to the right of pin *B* to work cloth stitch and twist, pin *j*, cloth stitch and twist. The right hand pair is the weaver, it works to the right through the four pairs from *a*, *b*, *c* and *d* with cloth stitch and twist. Put pin *k* to the left of the weaver, give it one twist extra and work back through five pairs to *m*. Twist the weaver once more and work back through four pairs (one pair less) to *n*, and return to *o*. It travels through three pairs to *p* and back to *q*, through two pairs to *r* and back to *S*. From *S* it travels to *T* through six pairs (five fan pairs and one from the ground). As the weaver is covering extra distance it looks better if it receives an extra twist. From *T* weave back to *U* through six pairs. From *U* to *s* work through two pairs, from *t* to *u* through three pairs, from *v* to *w* through four pairs and from *x* to *y* through five pairs. Finish work with cloth stitch and twist to cover pin *z*. The pair from *h* works cloth stitch through these two pairs at *z*. Pin *C* is put up to the right of the weaver, this is the cloth fan weaver.

The corner

Work the ground row from *S*. Work the cloth stitch and twist fan using the diagram as a guide. From *V* the weaver travels through six pairs to *X*, this includes the pair taken in for *T*.

If this pattern is transferred to a graph paper of ten squares to 2cm and Retors D'Alsace no. 30 used it makes an attractive edging for handkerchiefs or lingerie.

7 Plaited Laces

These are popular as they form pleasant curving patterns with more freedom than the narrow tape or geometric Torchon. Bedfordshire (Beds-Maltese) lace, a development from Maltese lace, is an elaboration of simple plaited lace. Recognized by a profusion of plaits, picots and leaves it is used for edgings and insertion, collars and cuffs as well as many decorative pieces for insertion, doyleys or mounting under glass.

Plait and leaf edging

To learn the plait, picot and leaf, the lace in photograph 65 is worked. To prepare the pricking, fig. 66, eight pairs of bobbins wound with Pearl cotton no. 12 are required. Refer to working diagram 67.

To begin the footside
Hang two pairs around *A* and two pairs side by side on *B*. Twist the right hand threads on *A* twice and work cloth stitch and two twists (twists on both bobbins) to cover the pin. Ignore the right hand pair and work the left hand pair through the two pairs on *B* in cloth stitch. Twist the weaver twice and put up pin *b* to the right of the weaver.

Footside sequence
Take the fourth pair (in this case the weaver) from the outside edge and work two cloth stitches towards the edge (the right edge). Twist the weaver twice, work cloth stitch and two twists with the outside edge pair and put up pin *c* to the left of both pairs. Ignore the outer pair and work the left hand pair back to the left through the two passive pairs in cloth stitch. Note that the passive pairs are untwisted.

Continue to practise until this sequence can be worked quickly without reference to instructions. Put up pin *d* to the right of the weaver and work to the footside pin *e*.

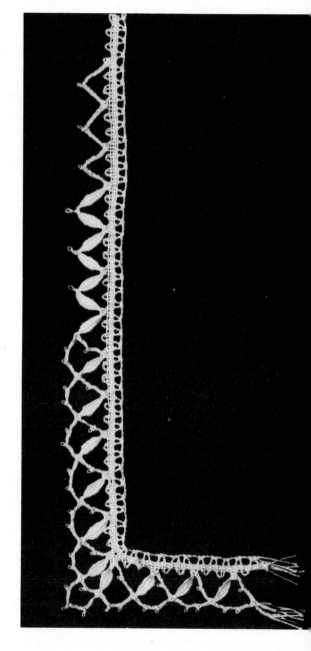

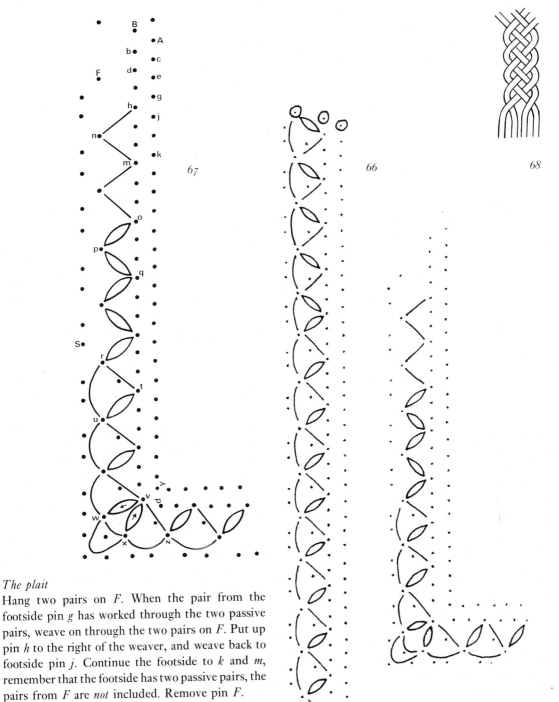

67

66

68

The plait

Hang two pairs on *F*. When the pair from the footside pin *g* has worked through the two passive pairs, weave on through the two pairs on *F*. Put up pin *h* to the right of the weaver, and weave back to footside pin *j*. Continue the footside to *k* and *m*, remember that the footside has two passive pairs, the pairs from *F* are *not* included. Remove pin *F*.

Refer to illus. 68 and use the four threads from *h* to make a half stitch. Continue to make half stitches until the plait is the required length. To achieve good tension the threads are pulled to the sides between each stitch.

The picot

At *n* this will be made to the left of the plait. Refer to illus. 69. Take the two left hand threads of the plait in the left hand and hold them taut. Take a pin in the right hand, put it under the right of these two threads, and pull the left thread across underneath it (*a*) so that the threads are crossed. Bring the pin towards the worker over the crossed threads, then turn the point of the pin away taking it under the crossed threads and up between them (*b*). Stick the pin into the picot hole to the left of the plait and ease the threads until a single picot thread appears about the pin (*c*). The threads must be manipulated until a single tight picot appears to the side of the plait.

A picot set to the right of the plait is made satisfactorily if instructions for the picot on the left are followed and the pin inclined into a hole on the right (*d*). Ascertain that the picot at *n* can be seen, and continue to plait in a straight line from *h*. When long enough incline it towards *m*, if the plait is made by pulling the threads towards *m* the picot will be pulled out of shape. The footside pin has worked from *k* and is ready to link in the plait at *m*.

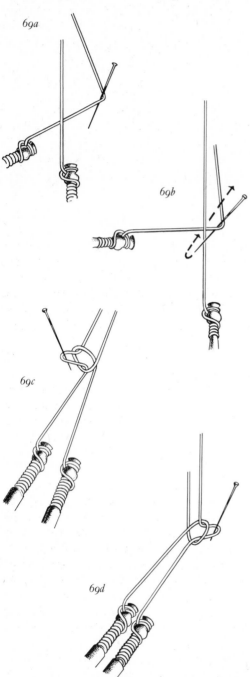

69a

69b

69c

69d

To link the plait to the footside

Refer to diag. 70 and take the weaver from the foot-side through both plait pairs in cloth stitch. Put up the pin (*m*) *between* the plait pairs (in this case leaving two pairs to the left of the pin) and cover the pin with the pairs on either side of it. The right hand pair from the pin (*m*) is the footside weaver and the other two pairs make the plait. Note that the weaver from the footside has become part of the plait and the left hand pair from the plait has become the new weaver. Practise making plaits, picots and the joining of plaits to the trail.

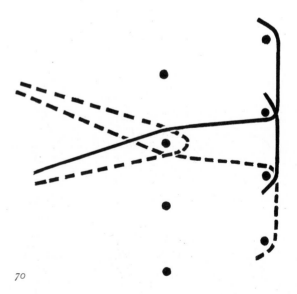

70

The leaf

Pairs from *o* make a leaf instead of a plait. Refer to illus. 71, make a cloth stitch and pull it up very tightly. Lengthen the thread which completed the stitch and take it under the right hand outside thread and back over it. Take it under the centre thread, over and back under the left hand thread and over the centre thread. Weaving continues in this way for the required length. Initially this is one of the most difficult techniques to master. The weaving thread must be kept neatly about the outside threads and controls the shape, therefore it must never hang unsupported or the leaf will be destroyed. At first it is necessary to keep the weaving close about the threads to achieve a pointed beginning. Gradually the outer threads are kept well apart and the weaver manipulated about them. At least three quarters of the leaf is worked before any adjustment is made to bring it to a point. The leaf is completed with cloth stitch made as follows: When the weaver comes from the left over the centre thread, work the other two moves as in the lower part of illustration 71.

Work a picot at *p*. Continue using the four threads to make another leaf. When it is complete incline it to *q*. Work the footside edge and join the leaf in as described for the plait join. Continue to practise.

The edging

Work the leaf to *r*, do not put in the pin. Hang two pairs around pin *S*. Normally pairs from position *S* will be plaited to *r*.

71

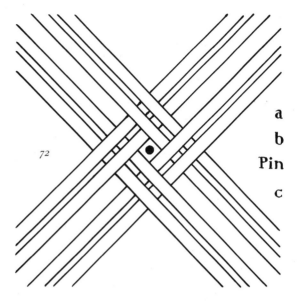

72

a
b
Pin
c

To cross plaits/leaves

Refer to illus. 72. Four pairs hang ready for use. Use each pair as a single bobbin is used in cloth stitch. Place the second over the third. At the same time take the fourth over the third and the second over the first. Put up the pin between the centre pairs. Place the second pair over the third. The plaits have crossed each other.

To continue

Plait from *r* to *t* and link the plait to the footside trail, work a leaf back to *u*. Plait from *r* to *u* making two picots to the left of the plait. Make a crossing at *u*. Continue.

The corner

Work normally to *v* and *w*. Plait from *w* to *x* and make a crossing. From *x* make a leaf to *v*. At *v* the footside weaver hangs from the pin, remove the pin and use the footside weaver to weave to the left through the leaf pairs from *x*. Replace the pin to the right of the weaver. Weave back through the leaf pairs and on through the two passive footside pairs. Remove pin *y*, work the outside edge stitch and use pin *y* a second time. Continue the footside to *d*. From *v* plait to *z*. In order to keep the pattern symmetrical the plaits will be made away from the footside and the leaves towards it. At the centre position between corners it will be necessary to work two leaves or two plaits to reverse the direction.

Pattern with plaits, leaves and half stitch diamonds

The lace in photograph 73 is worked from pricking 74 and requires twelve pairs of bobbins wound with Pearl cotton no. 12. Refer to working diagram 75.

73

74

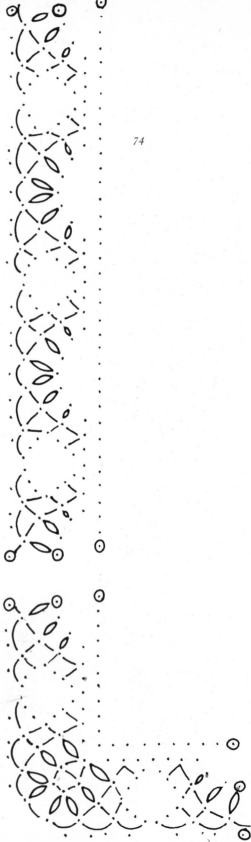

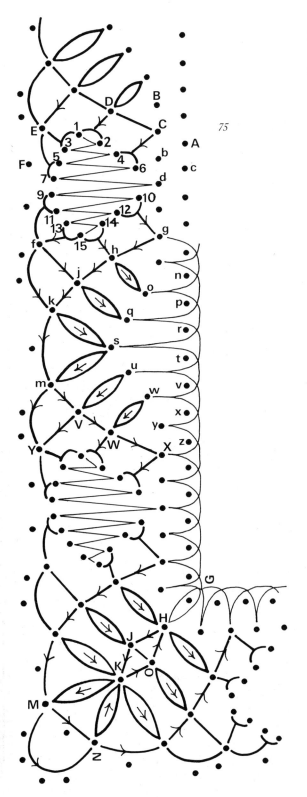

To begin the footside

Hang two pairs round pin *A* and two pairs side by side on pin *B*. Refer to the previous pattern if necessary and work from *A* to *b* and on to *d* but do not put in the pin at *d*.

The half stitch diamond

Hang three pairs side by side on *C*, one pair on *D*, two pairs on *E* and two pairs on *F*. Take the right hand pair from *E* and the pair on *D* and work half stitch, pin *1*, half stitch. Use the right hand pair to work to the right through the first pair on *C* in half stitch. Put up pin *2* to the left of the weaver and twist the weaver. Weave to the left through two passive pairs and through one from *E*. Put up pin *3* and twist the weaver. Remove support pin *D*. Weave to the right through three passive pairs and one from *C*, put up pin *4* and twist the weaver. Continue, weave through four passives and one from *F* for pin *5*, through five passives and one for pin *6*, through six passives and one for pin *7*, through seven passives to meet the footside weaver at *d*. Work cloth stitch and twist, pin *d*, cloth stitch and twist. Weave back through the same seven passives to pin *9*, through seven to pin *10*, through six to pin *11*, through five to pin *12*, through four to pin *13* and three to pin *14*. Weave back through two pairs, put up pin *15* and cover it. Check that the footside weaver is hanging from *d*, work the footside to *g*; check that one pair hangs from each pin *9* to *14* and two pairs only remain at *15*.

Plaits, leaves and cloth triangle

Pairs from *9* and *11*, *13* and *15*, *15* and *14*, and *12* and *10* make plaits. Remember the picot from the plait from *9* and work the crossing at *f*. The plait from *10* and *12* is linked to the footside at *g*. Continue to plait and make crossings at *h, j, k*, and work on to *m*. Make leaves from *h, j* and *k*. The cloth triangle is part of the footside. From the footside pin *n* work back through two passive footside pairs and on through the pairs from the leaf from *h*. Put up pin *o* to the right of the weaver. Work back through the new passive pairs and the footside passives to pin *p*. Weave back to include the pairs from pin *j* and put up pin *q*. Weave back through six pairs to footside pin *r*, and return through eight pairs (this includes the pairs from *k*). Weave through eight pairs to footside pin *t*, through six pairs to *u* and back to *v*, through four pairs to *w*

53

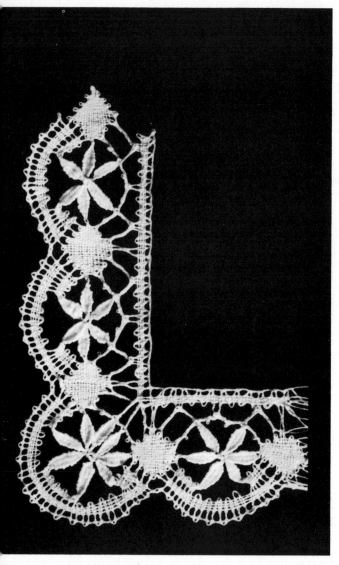

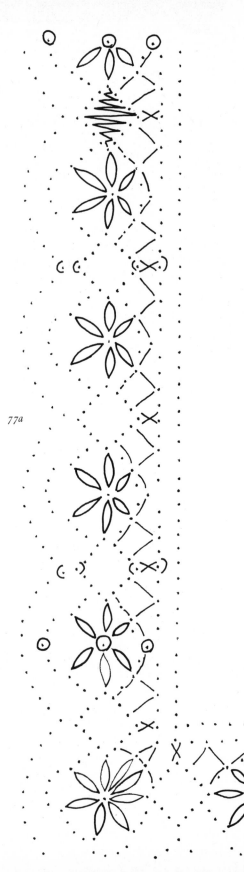

77a

and back to *x* and through the normal footside passives to *y* and *z*. Leaves are made from *s*, *u* and *w*. The plait from *k* and the leaf from *s* cross at *m*, the plait from *m* and leaf from *u* cross at *V*, the plait from *V* and leaf from *w* cross at *W*. Plaits from *m* and *V* cross at *Y* and the plait from *W* is linked to the footside trail at *X*. One repeat is complete, pairs are plaited to work the diamond, beginning with the right hand pair from *Y* and the left hand pair from *W*.

The corner
Work the corner pin *G* as a footside pin, and return through the two passive pairs to join in the leaf at *H*.

Leave the weaver hanging at H and plait the two pairs to J, a crossing is made with the leaf and the plait continues to make another crossing at K. Arrows on the diagram show the direction in which plaits and leaves travel. At K the left hand pairs make a leaf to M, plaits are made to N and the right hand pairs make a leaf back to K. Remove pin K, using the hanging pairs and the leaf pairs from N make the crossing and replace pin K. The right hand pairs plait to O and on to H. Remove pin H, use the footside weaver hanging at H to link in the pairs, replace pin H. The weaver works to the footside and uses the corner pin a second time. Leaves and plaits are made in preparation for the half stitch diamond.

Daisy pattern

The lace is shown in photo 76 as an edging with corner. It is illustrated in the frontispiece as a circular edging, the mat including lace has a diameter of 300mm (12 inches). By careful pattern matching an oval pricking can be made. Match the capped holes on the pricking, fig. 77a with the ringed holes on fig. 77b. The curved edging has fewer holes on the footside than the straight edging and illus. 78b shows the simplified working. For the straight edging prepare sixteen pairs of bobbins wound with Pearl cotton no. 12 and pricking 77a.

The footside
Refer to page 48 if necessary. Work to d and put up the pin.

The diamond
Five pairs enter on either side, hang these on support pins behind the diamond. The centre pairs work cloth stitch, pin f is put up and the pair to the left of the pin becomes the weaver. Weave to the right through the other pair at f and through one pair on a support pin, put up the pin and continue, bringing in one pair at each pin to g, put up the pin. The diamond weaver and the footside weaver each require three twists they work together with cloth stitch and three twists (on both bobbins). The weavers have changed position and now continue, the footside weaver becomes the diamond weaver and the diamond weaver works the footside. The diamond weaver works through one pair less at each pin until two pairs are left to cover pin k. Pairs from g

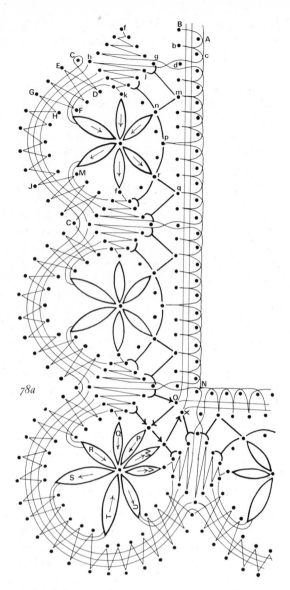

78a

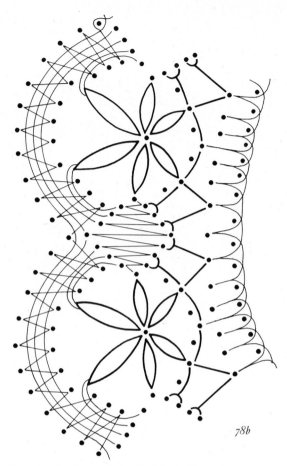

78b

and *j* plait to *m*, they are linked to the footside and plait to *n*. The next available pairs from the diamond plait to make a crossing at *n*. Remember the picot on this plait and the others on the curve to the next diamond.

The headside

On the left hang the remaining two pairs on *C* and cover the pin with cloth stitch and twist. Give the right hand pair an extra twist and weave through the next two pairs in cloth stitch, twist the weaver twice and work through two pairs more in cloth stitch. Twist the weaver twice and put up pin *D*. Return to

the outside edge and pin *E* with similar twists. Refer to the photograph to clarify the working (i.e. two cloth stitches, two twists, two cloth stitches, two twists and cloth stitch and twist with the edge pair). Work to *G*. Two pairs hang from pins *F*, *k* and *n* to make leaves. These are crossed and more leaves made to *M*, *f* and *r*.

Six plait crossing

Refer to illus. 79. Six pairs from leaves or plaits hang ready for use. Treat each pair as a single thread.

Take the right centre pair over the next pair to the right.

Take the left centre pair under the next pair to the left.

Cross the new centre pairs right over left. Put up a pin between them.

Take the pair to the right of the pin, out to the right, over the next and under the outside pair.

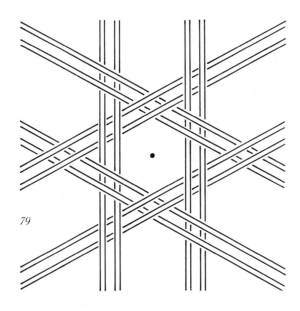

79

Take the pair to the left of the pin to the left under the next and over the outside pair.

Take the left centre pair under the next pair to the left.

Take the right centre pair over the next pair to the right.

Cross the new centre pairs right over left.

Take the right centre pair over the next pair to the right.

Take the left centre pair under the next pair to the left.

To continue the pattern

Put pin *f* between the pairs of the middle leaf, it is ready to begin the diamond. The plait from *n* is linked to the footside at *p*. As the footside weaver travels a greater distance, the lace will look more attractive if the weaver is twisted three times before the join is made and again three times before it travels back through the passive footside pairs. The right hand leaf makes a four plait crossing at *r* and the plaits are made to *q* and to the diamond. Weaving continues on the headside, there are three passives only, the cloth stitch and twist pair on the edge and the two cloth pairs. Weave to *H* and continue to *M*. From *J* there will be cloth stitch and twist, an extra weaver twist, two cloth stitches, two twists on the weaver and two cloth stitches through the leaf pairs.

Pin *M* is put up and the headside worked to pin *C*. Pairs are twisted once before entering the diamond.

The corner

Complete the diamond and work the footside weaver to the corner pin *N* but do *not* come back through the passive pairs. The left hand side passive from the footside works as the weaver to link in the plait at *O*. It makes one cloth stitch with the other passive to the right of it. Work the headside to release pairs for leaf *R*. Make leaves *R*, *Q* and *P* and work the six plait crossing. Make leaf *S* with the two left hand pairs and work the headside to take in the pairs and release them for leaf *T*. Make leaf *T*. Remove the centre crossing pin and work another six plait crossing using pairs from leaf *T* and the four pairs hanging from the pin. Re-use the pin hole. Make leaves *U*, *V* and *W*. The plait to the corner from leaf *W* is joined in using the second footside passive at *X* as shown in the diagram. There are two pairs to the right of corner pin *N*, take the inner (left) pair and work through the two footside passives to await the diamond weaver. Continue the headside to take in the pairs from leaf *U*.

The circular edging

There is no link between footside and diamond weaver pairs, the plaits are linked as in illus. 78b.

Half stitch triangle and leaf pattern

The pattern shown in photograph 80 is used also as part of an oval mat on page 77. Prepare sixteen pairs of bobbins with Fils a Dentelles no. 70 and pricking 81. Study the lace to try to understand how the threads are used, the headside is similar to the headside in the previous pattern. The footside has the usual passive pairs and links in plaits. However, the footside weaver also has links with the half stitch triangle. Refer to diagram 82.

To begin the footside

Hang two pairs on *A* and two pairs side by side on *B*. Twist the pairs on *A* and cover the pin with cloth stitch and twist. Take the left hand pair through the two passive pairs on *B*. Twist the weaver.

The half stitch triangle

Note that two plaits begin the triangle at *a*, both

pairs of the plait enter at pins *b*, *d* and *f* and single pairs at *h* and *k*. Hang one pair on pin *a*, three pairs side by side on *C*, four on *D* and four on *E*. The weaver on *a* works to the left in half stitch through the three pairs on *C* and through two pairs from *D*. Put up pin *b* to the right of the weaver and weave back through the five passive pairs to *c*. The weaver from the triangle and the weaver from the footside (fourth pair from the right hand side) work cloth stitch and twist, pin *c*, cloth stitch and twist. Put the right hand pair from pin *c* (foot weaver) and the three pairs to the right of it to one side. Take the left hand pair from pin *c* and weave back through the five passive pairs and two pairs more from *D*. Put up pin *d* and weave back through seven passive pairs to *e*. Remove pins *C* and *D* and ease the threads down. Weave through seven passive pairs and two from *E* to *f*. Weave back through nine pairs to *g*. Weave back through nine passive pairs and one from *E* to *h* and back through ten passive pairs to *j*. Work the footside to *j* and use the two weavers for cloth stitch and twist, pin *j*, cloth stitch and twist. Again put the four right hand pairs well to one side. Weave back to *k* through ten passives and the last pair from *E*. From *k* to *m* weave through eleven passive pairs, work the footside and join the weavers, work back through ten passives to *n*. Work through ten passives to *o*, continue through nine to *p* and back to *q*, through seven pairs to *r* and back to *s*, through five pairs to *t* and back to *u*. Put up pin *u* and cover with one half stitch. Remember to link with the footside at *s*.

Plaits

The pairs from *k* and *n* are plaited together. Plaits are made with pairs from *p*, *r*, *t* and *u* (two plaits).

Headside

Put pin *K* between the pairs of the left hand plait and cover with cloth stitch and twist. The right hand weaver pair works in cloth stitch to the right through two pairs from *p*, twist weaver once, through two pairs from *r*, twist weaver once and through the four pairs from *t* and *u*. Continue to *W*, keeping twists on the weaver to achieve the pattern feature. Two pairs from *w* make a leaf to *x*. Work the footside to link in the plait at *v*, continue to *y*. The leaf from *w* and plait from *v* cross at *x*. Plait the right hand pairs to *y* and link the plait in at once. Make the leaf to *z*. Continue

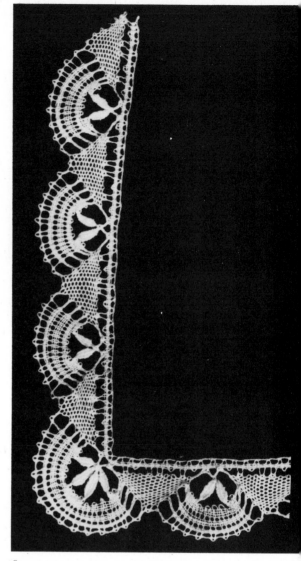

80

to work the head, include the leaf pairs from *z*, work to *Y*.

The pairs from *Y* make a short plait, plait the other pairs for the triangle. Plait the pairs from *y*. One repeat is complete.

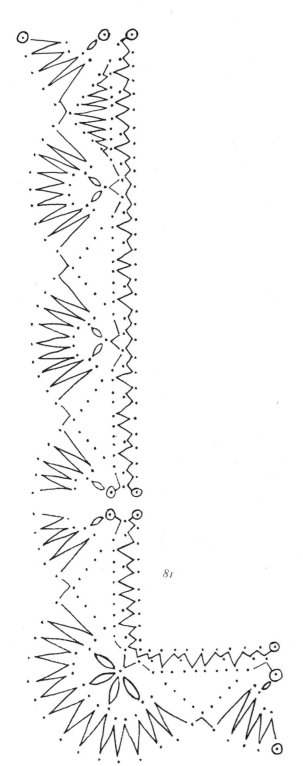

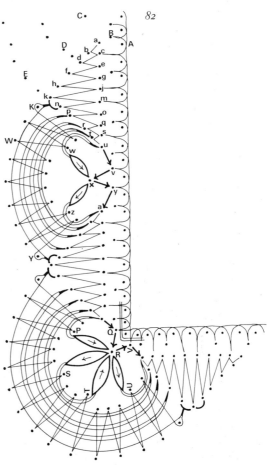

The corner

Refer to the working diagram. The leaf from P and plait from Q make a crossing at R. The left hand pairs make a leaf to S, the right hand pairs are left hanging from pin R. The headside working will include the leaf pairs as shown and release them for the leaf from T. The pin is removed and a second crossing made at pin R. The right hand pairs work a plait and are linked into the footside at V. The left hand pairs make a leaf to U and the headside is completed. Plaits are made to begin the triangle.

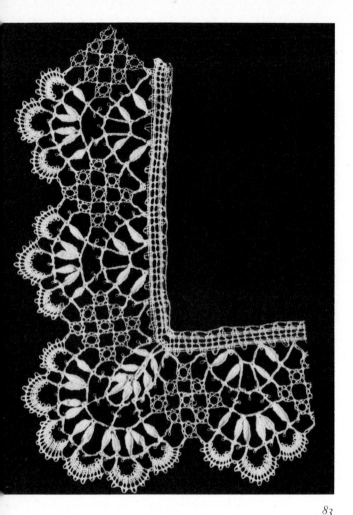

Rose ground and scallop pattern

Illustrated in photograph 83, this pattern combines the plaits and leaves with the Torchon rose ground feature explained on page 44. Prepare nineteen pairs of bobbins wound with Fils a Dentelles no. 70 and pricking 84a. Refer to working diagram 85.

The rose ground diamond
Hang two pairs on pins at *J, K, M, N, O* and *P*. Pairs from *M* and *N* work rose ground unit *1*. Remove pin *N*.

Pairs from *K* and left hand side of unit *1* work unit *2*.

Pairs from *J* and left hand side of unit *2* work unit *3*.

Remove pins *J, K* and *M*.

Pairs from the right hand side of unit *1* and *O* work unit *4*. Remove pin *O*.

Pairs from the right hand side of unit *2* and the left hand side of unit *4* work unit *5*.

Pairs from the right hand side of unit *3* and the left hand side of unit *5* work unit *6*.

Pairs from the right hand side of unit *4* and *P* work unit *7*. Remove pin *P*.

Pairs from the right hand side of unit *5* and the left hand side of unit *7* work unit *8*.

Pairs from the right hand side of unit *6* and the left hand side of unit *8* work unit *9*.

Plait pairs in preparation for the central pattern feature.

To begin the footside
As the space is wide five pairs of footside passives are used, these are arranged with a cloth stitch and twist pair in the centre. Refer to *basic stitch no. 4*, page 15. Hang two pairs on *A* and five pairs side by side on *P*. Twist the pairs on *A* and cover with cloth stitch and twist. Take the left hand pair from pin *A* through the passive pairs as follows. Cloth stitch through two pairs, twist the weaver once, cloth stitch and twist with the next pair, cloth stitch through two pairs. Put up pin *b*, twist the weaver twice.

Footside sequence
Use the seventh pair from the edge (in this case the weaver to the left of pin *b*). Work to the right with cloth stitch through two pairs, twist the weaver once, cloth stitch and twist through the next pair and cloth stitch through the two pairs remaining. Twist the weaver and work cloth stitch and twist with the outside edge pair. Put up pin *C* on the footside inside (to the left of) two pairs. Twist the outer pair once more and discard it. Take the other pair back through two cloth pairs, twist the weaver once, cloth stitch and twist, two cloth stitches, twist the weaver twice.

Leaves and plaits
Link the plait to the footside at *d*. Arrows on the diagram indicate the movement of pairs and the crossings are worked in letter order. Work crossings at *e* and *f* and the leaves to *g* and *h*. Link the leaf to the footside at *g* and make the crossing at *h*. The plait from *j* to *k* has picots on both sides. Work the picot on the left, use the pairs to make one half stitch and

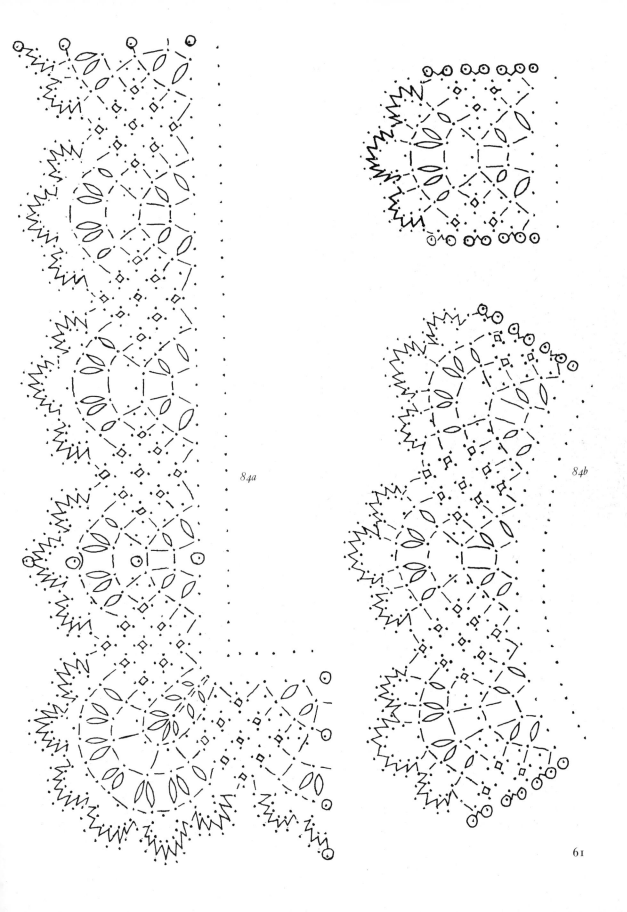

84a

84b

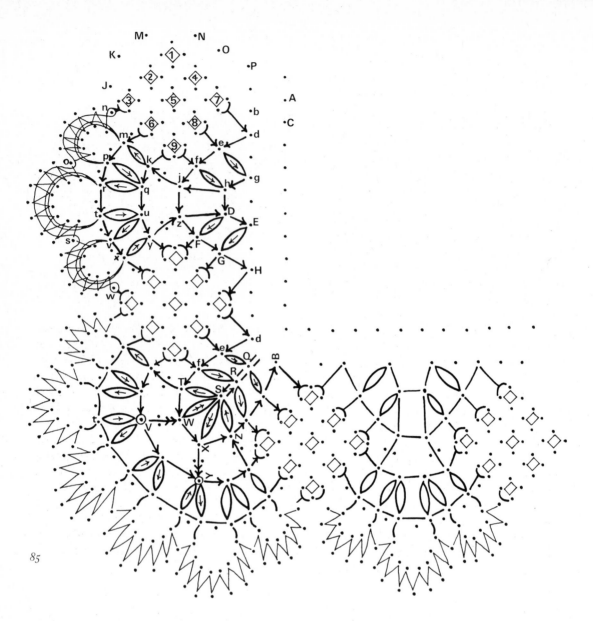

85

work the picot on the right. The half stitch avoids the appearance of a hole between picots. Work to *m* with a leaf from *k*. The left hand pairs from *m* make a short plait. At *n* the pin is put between plait pairs and covered with cloth stitch and twist. The right hand pair is weaver and works to the right in cloth stitch through the two plait pairs from *m*. A pin is put up to the left of the weaver and the scallop edge is worked. Take the weaver to the left through two pairs in cloth stitch, twist the weaver once and work cloth stitch and twist on the outside edge. The pin is put up to hold the weaver in position and the weaver works

back with cloth stitch and twist and two cloth stitches, work to *o*. The two cloth stitch pairs are plaited together again and back to *p*. Make certain that the cloth pairs are plaited and the weaver is at pin *o*. Work the crossing at *p* and the right hand pairs make a leaf to *q*. The left hand pairs from the crossing at *q* make a leaf back to *r*. Working from *r* to *t* is the same as the working from *m* to *p*. Continue in letter order to *z*. The right hand pairs from *z* cross at *D* the pairs from *h*. Continue in letter order to *H*.

The next rose ground diamond is worked with pairs from *w*, *x*, *y*, *F*, *G* and *H*.

The corner

Two extra pairs are required. Work to pin *f*. To work the foot refer to illus. 86. The weaver from *d* works to the right through two cloth pairs and the cloth stitch and twist pair. The pin is put in as shown and the weaver returns through the same pairs to the left. The weaver and the left side passive make a short plait to the crossing at *Q* with the leaf from *e*. A crossing is made at *R* with the leaf from *f*. The left hand pair from *R* plaits to *S*, a pin is put between the pairs and a leaf is made with the same pairs to *T*. The left hand pairs are plaited and work the normal edging to *V*. The extra pairs are joined in with a six plait crossing (refer to page 57) at *V*. Use the leaf pairs from *t*, the plait pairs from *v* and the extra pairs hung on a support pin (possibly the picot pin near *T*). Work the crossing and remove support pin. The left hand pairs make a leaf and continue the scallops to *Y*. The centre pairs plait for normal use. The right hand pairs plait and travel as indicated by double arrows to *W* where they cross the plait from *T*. The left hand pairs plait to *X* and the right hand pairs make a leaf to *S*. The pairs are twisted either side of the pin and another leaf is made to the crossing at *X*. The right hand pairs plait to *Z* and the left hand pairs plait to *Y* for a six plait crossing. Two pairs are knotted and discarded. The other pairs continue the scallop edging. A leaf is made from *Z* to *S*. The pin at *S* is removed and a small hook put through the two holes formed by twisted threads. Hook two of the leaf threads through and pass the other two through the loop. Pull firmly and tie one knot to hold them in position. Plait to *R* and remove the pin. Use the plait pairs and hanging pairs to work

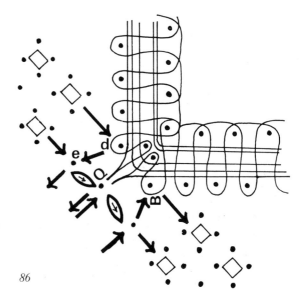

86

a four plait crossing and replace pin *R*. Repeat this at *Q* and make a short plait with the right hand pairs. The right pair of the plait weaves to the right through one cloth passive pairs and one pair in cloth stitch and twist, the pin is put up and it works back through one pair in cloth stitch and twist and two pairs in cloth stitch (this includes the left hand pair from the plait) to pin *B*. Written instructions appear very complicated, close reference to the working diagrams simplifies the making of the lace. From *B* the footside corner pin is used a second time.

To make a circular mat six repeats of pricking 84b are required to be set on a circle of radius 95mm (3¾ inches). If the extra single pattern – or multiples of that pattern – are added on opposite sides an oval mat can be made.

8 Braids and Trimmings

All braids and trims should be simple and quick to make. Experiment is usually necessary to match threads, colours and pricking to achieve the desired effect. However, the lace maker who works the selection in this chapter should be able to make his/her own prickings and original braids.

The eight patterns given here are all worked with Pearl cotton no. 8, each pricking is set on a grid so that it can be reduced or enlarged according to thread available. They are shown in colour on the book cover.

Pattern 1

Photograph 87 and pricking 88. Approximately nine pairs of bobbins, depending on closeness required, are used.

Hang one weaver pair on a pin at *A* and all other passive pairs on support pins behind the work. Work through all pairs in cloth stitch to *B*. (If necessary refer to practice strip on page 14.) From *B* work in half stitch using the cloth stitch and twist edge as far as *a*. Continue.

Pattern 2

Photograph 89, diagram 90 and pricking 91. Ten pairs of bobbins are required. The pairs are used to make the diamond as in pattern on page 38. Two pairs are joined in on either side of the point. The weavers for the twisted scallop edging come from the bottom of the diamond and work out to the edge. Finally they return to the centre to begin the next diamond.

Pattern 3

Photograph 92, pricking 93 and diagram 94. Ten pairs of bobbins are required (refer to the diagram but ignore the small letters). Using three passive

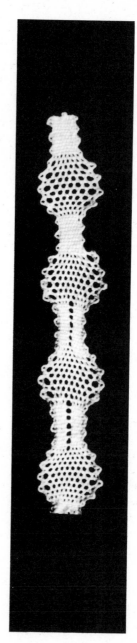

87

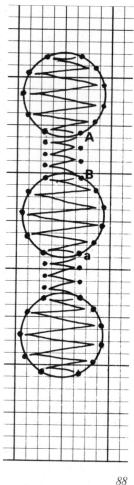

88

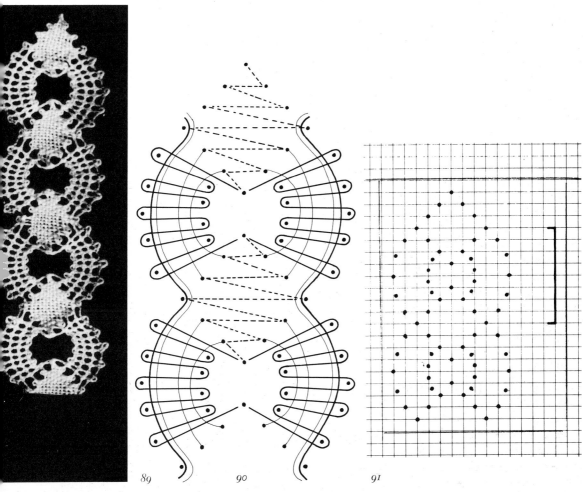

89   90   91

pairs and one weaver pair on each side weave from *A* and *B* to *O*. Work the weavers together with cloth stitch, put up pin *O* and cover with cloth stitch. Take the weavers back to the outer edges and leave them at *C* and *D*. The three passive pairs from the trail from *A* cross through the three pairs from the trail from *B* in cloth stitch (if necessary refer to the first half of the spider on page 40.) Weavers from *C* and *D* work to the centre, meet with cloth stitch, pin *X*, cloth stitch and continue. If coloured pairs are introduced at the edges they remain with the weavers at pins *C* and *D* and do not take part in the crossing.

Pattern 4

An adaptation of pattern 3; photograph 95, pricking 93 and diagram 94. Hang weavers on *A* and *B* and make half stitch trails, the coloured threads remain on the cloth stitch and twist edge. The centre is worked half stitch pin *O*, half stitch and the weavers taken back to *C* and *D*. Trail pairs cross through each other in half stitch. Weavers from *C* and *D* work to the centre and *X* is worked as *O*.

To work the rose ground centre
Leave out pairs at *a*, *b*, *c* and *d*. Refer to page 44 for rose ground instructions. Take pairs back into the trails at *e*, *f*, *g* and *h*.

To work the leaf
Leave out pairs at *j* and *k*. Twist each three times and work half stitch before pin *y*. Make a leaf, put up pin *z* and cover with half stitch. Twist three times before taking pairs back into the trails at *m* and *n*.

65

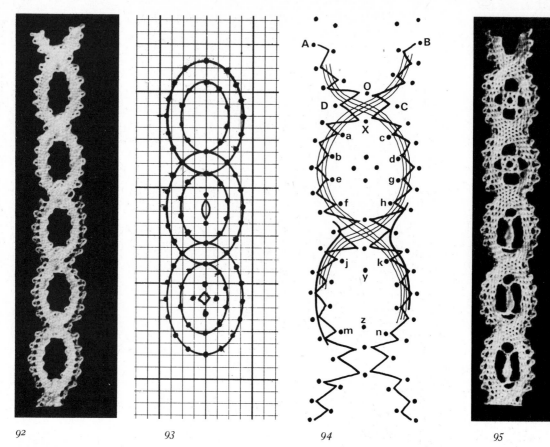

92   93   94   95

Pattern 5

Photograph 96, pricking 97 and diagram 98. Ten pairs of bobbins are required, two pairs in colour. Hang white pairs on support pins and work the rose ground unit *a*, *b*, *c*, *d*. Hang two white pairs on *e* and work cloth stitch and twist to cover the pin. Hang one coloured pair on a support pin and use the left hand pair from *e* to work cloth stitch and twist, pin *f*, cloth stitch and twist. Take the white weaver pair to work cloth stitch and twist, pin *g*, cloth stitch and twist with the edge passive pair. Work the coloured pair at *f* to the left in cloth stitch through the pairs from *cd* at position *h*. There is no pin at *h*. Take the weaver at *g* and work *i*, *j* *k* and *e*, there should be one cloth and twist pair at the edge and two cloth pairs inside.

Work similarly on the other side of the pattern. Use the coloured threads to make the tally, refer to page 33. Take the coloured pairs out towards the edges through pairs from *k* and *r* at *u* and *t*. There are no pins at *u* and *t*. The centre white pairs make the rose ground unit. Continue.

Pattern 6

Photograph 99, pricking 100 and diagram 101. Ten pairs of bobbins. This lends itself to work in colour. Hang two pairs on pins at *a*, *b* and *c* and cover each pin with half stitch. Hang three pairs on *d*. Twist the outside two threads twice. Take the right hand threads as weavers and work cloth stitch and twist twice through the other pairs on that pin. These are the footside pair and the passive twisted pair. The left hand weaver pair from *d* and a pair from *c* work half stitch, pin *h*, half stitch. Introduce a new pair from a support pin to work pin *e*. *f* and *g* are also worked as pin *h*. The pair from *h* works the footside and pin *n*. Work *j*, *k* and *m* with half stitch, pin, half stitch. The diagram shows extra stitches, pairs from *k* and *m*, and pairs from *j* and *k* work half stitches without pins to improve the appearance of the cloth stitch. The weaver from *n* (be certain that this has completed the footside sequence and has passed through the twisted edge passive pair) works six cloth stitches, the weaver is twisted three times

66

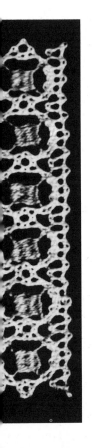

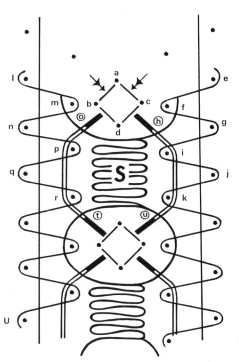

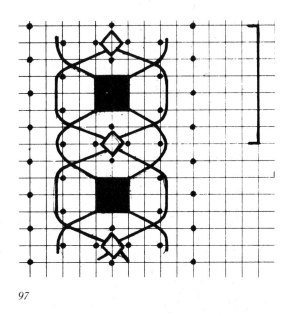

97

98

96

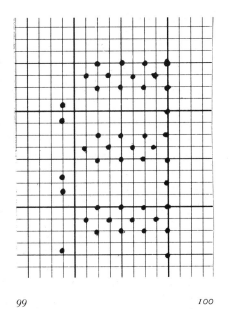

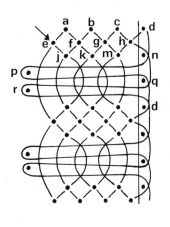

99

100

101

67

and the last pair is worked with cloth stitch and twist, pin p, cloth stitch and twist. Two additional twists are added before it returns with six cloth stitches towards the footside. The torchon footside sequence is worked and pin q is in position. Work from q to d as from n to q. Two pairs either side of centre are worked together in half stitch as at the beginning of the cloth stitch area. Twist the other pairs before working the half stitch pins.

Pattern 7

Photograph 102, pricking 103 and diagram 104. Nine pairs of bobbins. The pattern is particularly attractive in colour. Hang two pairs at B and two pairs at C, also five pairs in order on A. At A work the left hand two threads as weaver through the other four pairs. Twist the weaver once and the last passive pair once. Work cloth stitch and twist to cover pin B and cross the two weavers (second and third pairs from the right) with cloth stitch and twist (no pin). Cover pin C with cloth stitch and twist and work through the next three pairs in cloth stitch. Bring the left hand foot weaver through its passive pair and work this and the edge weaver together at D. The edge weaver continues to work the scallop edge in letter order, E, F, G, H, I, J, K and N. Work pin L and cross the weavers between the passive twisted pairs. The left hand weaver passes through its passive pair with cloth stitch and twist and works with the edge weaver at N. It is essential to follow the diagram and easier to work if the weavers are left in a central position between the passives, if necessary mark the weaver bobbins.

Pattern 8

Photograph 105, pricking 106 and diagram 107. Fourteen pairs of bobbins are required. The foot weavers and passives are common to both sides, the pattern should present no difficulties when pattern 7 is understood.

Preparing original designs
The following facts should be remembered:

(i) Half stitch, pin, half stitch – continues the colour diagonally.

(ii) Cloth stitch and twist, pin, cloth stitch and twist – the colours remain in the same position.

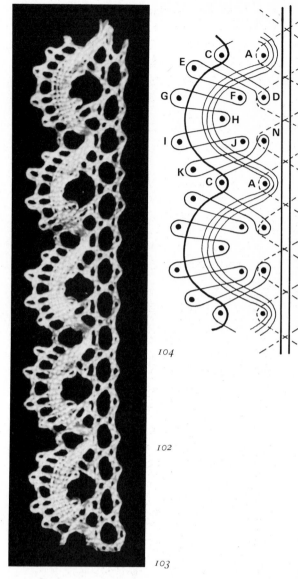

104

102

103

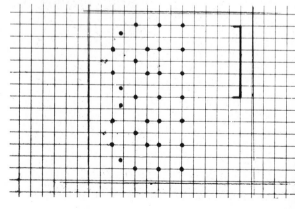

68

(iii) Pairs worked in cloth stitch and twist either on the edge or in the centre of half stitch retain their vertical position.

(iv) Plaits and leaves can be taken directly through trails and the colour retained, provided that the weaver is the colour of the leaves and plaits.

(v) The use of one coloured thread in a leaf, as leaf weaver, creates a coloured leaf and the other threads can be used as required in the braid.

(vi) Thick threads can be used for gimps, chain or corded, and two colours give added variety. Thick threads also make strong leaves or tallies and emphasize a particular colour.

(vii) The edge passive pair can be used as a gathering thread, it is better left untwisted.

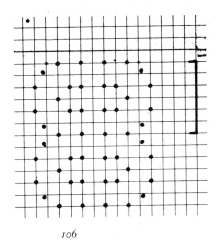

106

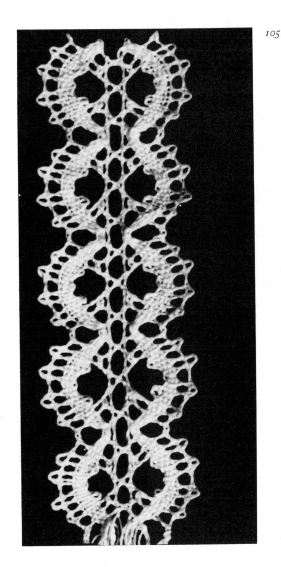

105

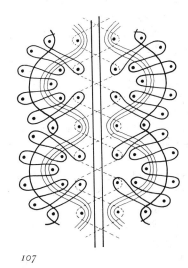

107

9 Mounting Lace

Although a book of samples and a collection of unmounted pieces of lace may prove that a person has mastered the basic techniques, they do not make anyone a lace maker. It is necessary to practise and experiment, but also important to experience the satisfaction of completing lace that can be used and admired. Lace is attractive on table or bed linen, on handkerchiefs or lingerie. Once again it is fashionable on blouses and dresses and popular on children's clothes. A custom made braid will enhance upholstery or a lampshade as threads can be selected to achieve the desired texture and colour. Lace in paperweights, trinket boxes and picture frames make original gifts and in brooches, pendants and earrings can be an expression of individuality. Patterns can be reduced by some modern photocopiers and worked with finer thread, and Torchon patterns can be adapted to specific requirements using graph papers and suitable thread.

Thread and fabric, especially ecru linens, need to be matched and it is worthwhile to purchase both before starting to make the lace. Consideration must be given to the weight of fabric as well as the shade. Similarly it is advisable to match the small lace motif with a suitable mount. The lace must fit well within the frame and always looks better if a border of the background fabric is visible. Lace under glass paper weights appears distorted if too near to the edge. The 'bull's eye' paperweight is unsuitable as it magnifies the motif and is unattractive.

The edging or insertion joined to form a circle, rectangle or square must be sewn securely. Pin the beginning of the lace onto the pricking so that the last repeat is worked to meet and no pins remain unworked. The final position of the pairs is obvious but care is needed to maintain the correct number of twists (illustration 108). Use a small hook to pull one thread through the hole made when the lace was started, and pass the other thread through this loop.

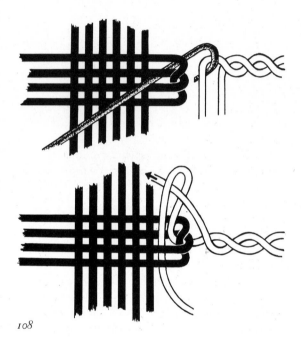

108

Pull both into position and tie one knot to hold it firmly. When all threads are fastened, cut off the bobbins leaving at least 100mm (4 inches) thread and take out the pins to remove the lace from the pillow. Lay the threads along the edge of cloth or a gimp thread and roll them together. Use one thread to oversew the others firmly to the lace. A roll of threads on the wrong side is preferable to lace which falls apart when laundered. Lace to be mounted can be finished in the same way, or as it is not handled the threads can be cut off close to the knots.

There are many ways of sewing the lace to the fabric. Three sided stitch is suitable in most situations, it can be used on fine fabric and equally well on coarse linen when threads are counted. It is an easy way of mounting lace on a curved edge. Refer to illustration 109. Work on the right side of the fabric. Lace thread can be used. Bring the needle out at *A*.

Put the needle in at *B* and out at *A* (back stitch).

Put the needle in at *B* and out at *A* (second back stitch).

Put the needle in at *C* and out at *A*.

Put the needle in at *C* and out at *D*.

Put the needle in at *C* and out at *D*.

Put the needle in at *C* and out at *D*.

Put the needle in at *A* and out at *D*.

Put the needle in at *A* and out at *a*.

Each time there are two stitches made. The back of the fabric can be cut away. It may be possible to overcast or blanket stitch the raw edge on the wrong side to avoid fraying if the fabric is loosely woven. When attaching the lace the footside edge is incorporated under the three sided stitch, the passive pairs should remain visible.

If lace is placed under glass permanently it is possible to avoid knots and oversewing in order to achieve a perfect appearance. However, the lace cannot be removed and used elsewhere later. When all the pins are in position, tie the ends of plaits and leaves with single knots so that they maintain good shape. When trails are complete hook the weaver through the first pin hole so that tension is achieved. Cut off the bobbins leaving at least 150mm (6 inches) of thread. Ascertain that the threads are in small groups. Remove the pins and transfer the motif to the backing material. This is not cut to size yet. Use a crewel needle to take the threads to the back of the

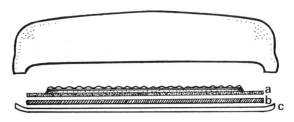

110

fabric. When the lace is neat and the ends are flat on the back, place it face downwards and lay a piece of iron-on interfacing over the threads. Press firmly, this traps the threads and stiffens the fabric, avoiding frayed edges and making it easier to handle. Cut the fabric to size, it should lie within the depression in the paperweight. Refer to illus. 110. Cut a second piece of fabric the same size, it is easier to handle if stiffened. Cut a piece of clear adhesive book or shelf covering 8mm ($\frac{1}{4}$ inch) larger all round. Peel the backing from the clear plastic and assemble as follows. Place the mounted lace (*a*) in the depression. Put the second piece of backing fabric (*b*) on top with the wrong sides of each piece touching. Put the adhesive plastic (*c*) on top so that it sticks to the edges of the glass. Turn it over to check that the lace is in the correct position. Press the plastic from the centre outwards, to exclude air and stick firmly at the edges. Use a craft tool or razor blade to trim away excess plastic. Use can be made of the felt backed adhesive covering. Two pieces are required, a smaller piece for mounting the lace and a larger piece to stick it to the glass.

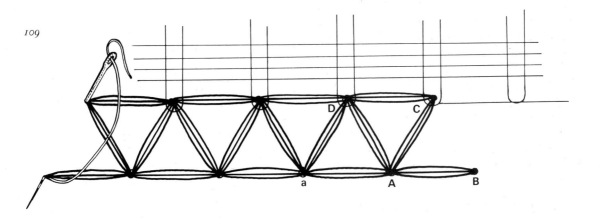

109

10 Twenty Patterns for Pleasure

The twenty patterns in this final chapter depend on the techniques mastered in the previous chapters. Full instructions are not included but details to assist the lace maker are given. It is recommended that the photograph and pricking are studied carefully and particular attention is paid to marking the pricking accurately. The use of clear plastic to facilitate working circular motifs is essential (refer to page 17).

Many of the patterns require fine thread, details are given with each pattern. Double picots are necessary when using Retors D'Alsace nos 30 and 50, Dewhurst's Sylko or any fine thread. Refer to illustration 111 and work as follows:

Picot on the left side
Take the two left hand threads of the plait, and twist three times. Take a pin in the right hand and hold it – point to the left – over the extreme left thread. Bring the point under the thread towards the worker and over into the picot hole (111a). Keep it loosely about the pin. Take the other thread and put it around the same pin, bringing it to the front and clockwise behind (111b). Twist the two threads together three times more and pull tightly together, they should form a cord around the pin. Practice is necessary, the threads do not cord if each is pulled as it goes round the pin.

Picot set to the right side
Twist the two right hand threads of the plait three times. Take a pin in the right hand and hold it – point to the left – under the right hand thread, bring the point over towards the worker and into the picot hole (112a). Take the other thread and bring it in front and behind the pin in an anti-clockwise direction (112b). Twist three times and pull together. When picots are worked on either side of a plait, a half stitch is worked between them to avoid an unsightly hole.

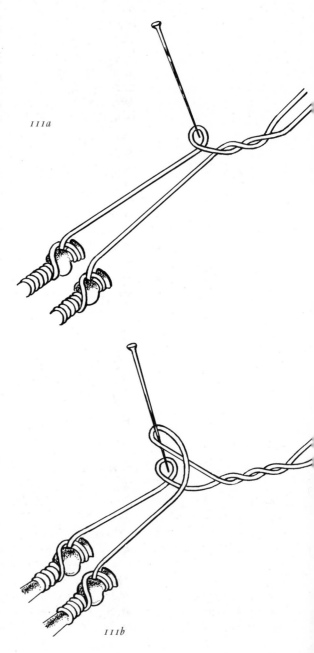

111a

111b

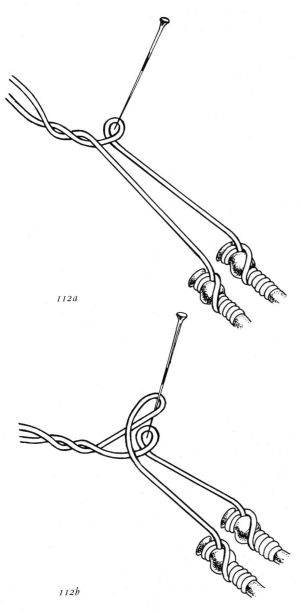

112a

112b

Pattern 1

Photograph 113, pricking 114 and diagram 115.

Thread

DMC Fils a Dentelles, nine pairs for fan and triangle edging, six pairs for leaves and plaits and five pairs for the inner footside trail.

References

Torchon fan, page 35.
Triangles, page 58.
Leaves, page 51.

Plaits, page 49.
Picots, page 72.
To link pairs to edge, page 50.
Six plait crossing, page 57.
Inner trail, page 48.
To complete lace, page 70.

Method

Work the fan and triangle edge first and link in the leaves and plaits later. Hang three pairs on a support pin at *B* and a weaver at *A*. Hang three more pairs on support pins ready for the triangle. Work the cloth triangle as far as position *z*. Place two pairs round a pin at *D* and cover with cloth stitch and twist. Work through four more pairs to *e*, work to *E*, to *f* and continue the Torchon twisted fan linking the fan and edge weavers with cloth stitch and twist, pin *z*, cloth stitch and twist. Complete the fan. Work the edging and make a neat join. Work the centre by hanging three pairs on a support pin and two on the footside. The pricking indicates the starting position. Join in two pairs to make the leaf on this trail and hook in two pairs on the cloth triangle edge, also to make a leaf. Hang two pairs on a support pin to fall between these leaves and make a six plait crossing. Remember to remove the support pin. Work the leaves and plaits, hooking in on the left and joining into the trail, work the footside trail as required.

Pattern 2

Photograph 116 and pricking 117.

Thread

DMC Fils a Dentelles. Twelve pairs for the edging and seven for the trail. Both parts are worked at the same time.

References

Hooking weaver into adjacent edge, page 70.
Edging, page 58.

Method

Begin the inner trail at *a* working in the direction of the arrow. Work triangle *b*, joining the weavers as shown in the pricking. Work leaves and fan and complete triangle *c*. Leave the edging and continue the inner tape trail changing to half stitch as shown in photograph. Ignore the plaits until the ringed hole

114

115

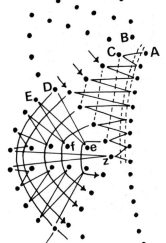

d is reached. At *d* take the weaver and the twisted edge pair and plait and picot to *x*. Give extra twists about the pin and plait and picot to *e*. Link the plait to the trail with a hook. Work back to *x*, twist the plait pairs once extra and work to *f*, to *x*, to *g* and back to *x*. This is the last time that the plait goes to *x*, remove the pin and put a hook through all the holes in the plait. Draw one of the plait pairs through and push the other through the loop. Pull carefully to achieve a neat centre and use a thread from each pair to tie one knot to hold it in position. Replace the pin and plait back to *d*. Continue the half stitch trail. Whenever the pairs are used to make a plait the hole is ringed to indicate the starting point.

75

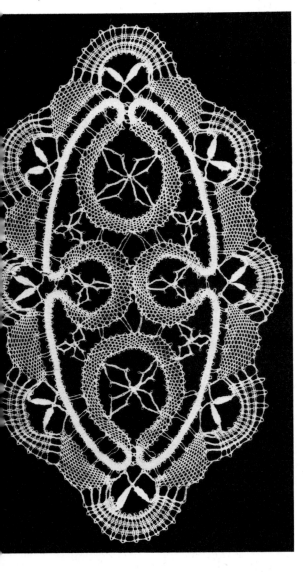

pairs for leaves at *a*, *b*, *c* and *d* and work the leaves. To begin the half stitch centre, put up a pin between the pairs of the leaf from *c*. The left pair is weaver and weaves through the other pair and on through the pairs of the leaf from *b*. The pin is put up and the weaver then includes the pairs from the leaf from *d*, and then from *a*. Pairs are discarded for the other four leaves, the pins are always covered and the last pin hole is covered with half stitch. Make the four leaves and continue the trail, taking in leaf pairs at the appropriate pin holes.

Additional information

To add pairs at the edge of a trail when they are used immediately for a leaf or plait, hang the two new pairs on a support pin and take the trail weaver through the two threads to one side of the pin with cloth stitch. Put up the pin and weave back through the same two threads and on through the trail. Remove the support pin and use the pairs for a plait or leaf. To join pairs to the trail and discard them at once is practical only when the work is for decoration and not to be laundered. Treat each pair from the plait or leaf as a single thread and take the trail weaver through with one cloth stitch. Put up the pin, lay the extra pairs to one side and continue the trail. The threads are knotted in pairs, the outer threads and the inner threads separately, leave at least 100mm (4 inches) thread and cut off the bobbins.

Pattern 3

Photograph 118 and pricking 119. Patterns 3 and 4 are suitable for an oval brooch mount.

Thread

DMC Retors D'Alsace no. 50. Four pairs for the edge and eight pairs for the leaves.

Method

Begin the edge trail at the ringed hole using one weaver pair and three passives, work in direction of arrow. Maintain two cloth pairs and one twisted pair on the edge. Join, on the inner cloth side of trail two

118

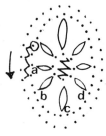

119

Pattern 4

Photograph 120, pricking 121 and diagram 122.

Thread
Retors D'Alsace no. 50. Eight pairs for the edge and ten for the centre.

References
Four plait crossing, page 51. Six plait crossing, page 57.

Method
Many motifs are worked from top to bottom. To begin turn the pillow and pricking upside down and refer to diag. 122. Hang two pairs on *q* and six pairs on *f*. All pairs hang round the pin so that adjacent threads belong to different pairs. Twist the two threads to the right of *q* three times and work through the six threads hanging to the left of *f*, work two cloth stitches and cloth stitch and twist for the outside edge. Put up pin *r* to the right of the weaver. Take the left hand threads from *q* and work two cloth stitches and cloth stitch and twist through the same six threads. Put up pin *j* to the left of the weaver. Remove support pin *f* and turning the pillow as necessary, continue the edge trail on either side, *r*, *s* and *t*, also *j*, *k* and *m*. Turn the pillow round so that this working is at the top. Eight pairs for four plaits are added as indicated on the pricking. At the point where the top plaits meet, two pairs are added at the six plait crossing. Work the half stitch centre, begin with a pin between the pairs of the centre plait and bring in one pair of the plait at each hole. Leave out similarly. Complete the plaits and trails taking in the plaits as described on page 77. It is usual to knot adjacent threads on one side trail and to anchor the weaver only securely on the other. When the work is mounted the loose threads can be placed in the best position to give the appearance of continuity.

Pattern 5

Photograph 123 and pricking 124. Suitable for brooch or pendant, including crown mount.

Thread
Retors D'Alsace no. 50. Ten edge pairs and fourteen pairs for the centre.

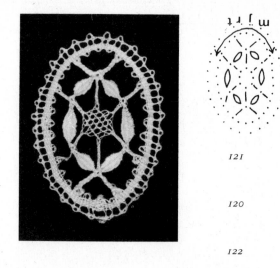

121

120

122

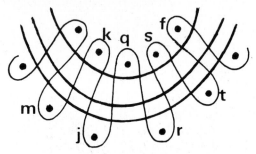

123

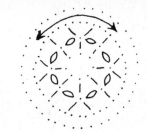

124

Reference
Pattern 4.

Method
Worked similarly to the previous pattern, but one pair extra is twisted on the inner edge of the trail. At the centre side pins in the half stitch centre the weaver is taken out, well twisted, linked to the four plait crossing and brought back to the centre.

Pattern 6

Photograph 125, pricking 126 and diagram 127. Suitable for brooch or pendant.

Threads
Retors D'Alsace no. 50. Six pairs of bobbins.

Reference
Scallop edged pattern, page 60.

Method
The pattern consists of two concentric plaits and a third which works the edge plaits, crosses the outer circle plait, works leaves to the inner plait and continues. The pattern is easy to understand but the skill lies in the use of fine thread. Hang pairs behind the work and join in four pairs at the ringed pin hole with a four plait crossing. The right hand plait moves as shown by the arrow and the other plait makes a leaf to *x*. Two more pairs are added at the four plait crossing at *x* and the plaits continue.

126

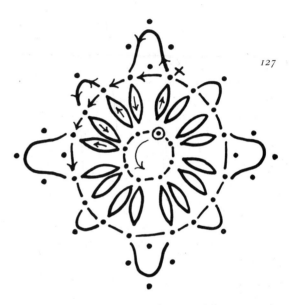

127

125

Pattern 7

Photographs 128a and b, pricking 129 and diagram 130. Suitable for brooch or pendant.

Thread
Retors D'Alsace no. 50. Six pairs and four extra for the plait/leaf effect in the centre.

Method
Begin with a plait crossing at the ringed hole, plait the left hand pairs to *x* and join in two more pairs. The left hand pairs continue the outer edge and the inner pairs plait to *o* where two pairs are added for the centre leaf/plait effect. Two more pairs are added at *p* and as the work progresses pairs are left out at *r* and *s*.

128a

128b

Pattern 8

Photograph 131 and pricking 132. Suitable for large
earrings or any ring of 50mm (2 inch) diameter.
Prickings can be made to fit any available ring.

Thread

DMC Fils a Dentelles or mercerized cotton no. 40
(Dewhurst's Sylko). Six pairs for the pattern and an
additional eight pairs for the centre leaves.

Method

Put the ring over the pricking and put one pin in
each hole outside to hold it in position. Begin at the
ringed hole with a six plait crossing, the right pairs
make the centre leaf, the centre pairs begin the
circular plait and the left hand pairs plait to *b* where
two more pairs are added at a four plait crossing.
Arrows indicate the direction of working, and
additional leaf pairs are joined in at six plait
crossings at *a*, *d* and *e*. At point *x* and seven similar
points the plaits are linked to the ring. Remove the
pin and with a hook pull two of the four plait threads
under the ring. Pass the other two threads through
the loop and pull up tightly. Manipulate the threads
and bobbins so that they lie evenly together at the
inside of the ring. Tie a knot to hold them in
position, replace the pin and continue. The leaves
from the ringed hole and from *a*, *d* and *e* make an
eight plait crossing (see below) and four more leaves
are worked to *f*, *g*, *h* and *j*. Knots may appear

129

130

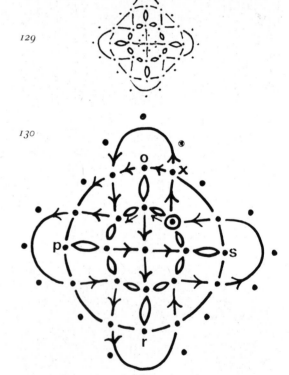

unsightly, the following is suggested as an alternat-
ive. Work the six plait crossing and take six threads
for each plait. Use two single threads and two double
threads to provide the four required. Discard the
extra threads from the plait, they can be trimmed
closely later.

80

131

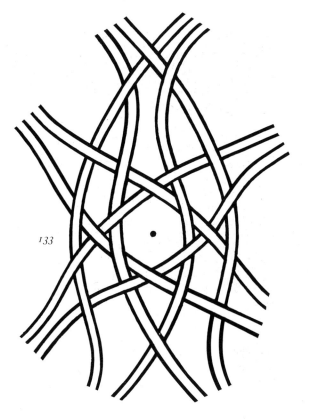

133

132

Eight plait crossing

Refer to illus. 133. Use the four plait/leaves as eight pairs. Use each pair as a single bobbin. Centre four pairs work half stitch. The right hand four pairs work half stitch. The left hand four pairs work half stitch. Repeat these three moves. Put up a pin in the centre, the centre pairs work cloth stitch. On the left, cross the centre pairs left over right. On the right, cross the centre pairs left over right.

Pattern 9

Photograph 134 and pricking 135.

Thread

Retors D'Alsace no. 30 or mercerized sewing cotton no. 40. Four pairs for the edge, two for the leaves which are worked round the motif and six for the leaves which work to the centre and out again.

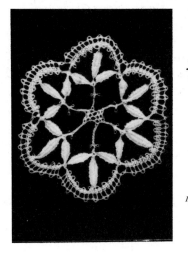

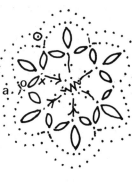

134   *135*

Method

Begin the trail at the ringed hole with the weaver and three pairs of passive threads (two in cloth stitch and the outer pair as a cloth stitch and twist edge). Add two pairs for a leaf at the centre of the curve as indicated. Stop at pin *a* with a cloth stitch and twist covering the pin. The first leaf is worked and new pairs are added at *x* for the leaf which travels around the circle linking with the outside edge. Make this leaf towards *o*, plait the cloth edge pairs with two half stitches only and make a four plait crossing. The right hand pairs make a leaf immediately and the left hand pairs are plaited for a short distance and then become the cloth passive pairs on the edge again. Three leaves/plaits work to the centre; the half stitch is completed; the pairs work out for the other half.

Pattern 10

Photograph 136 and pricking 137.

Thread

Retors D'Alsace no. 50. Four pairs for the scallop edging. Three passive pairs and a weaver for each trail, and six pairs for leaves.

Reference

Braid no. 7, page 68.

Method

Study the pricking. The trails are worked independently and linked as shown when the weavers meet to make tallies. Always continue the trail *without* the tally weaver first, this helps to maintain the tally shape. Begin the outer trail from the ringed dot, at the large dot join in two extra pairs for the scallop, refer to the scallop braid for the working of this edge. Begin the inner trail and work tallies as required. Join in three leaves, work the centre and the second half of the motif.

Pattern 11

Photograph 138 and pricking 139.

Thread

Retors D'Alsace no. 30 or mercerized sewing cotton no. 40. Four pairs for the edging and leaves, two for each circular plait and four for the centre leaves.

136

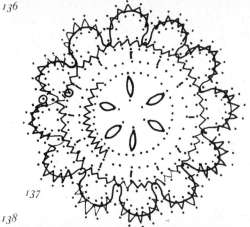

137

138

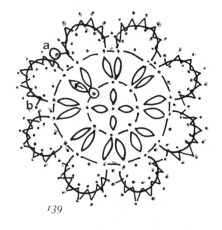

139

140

Reference
Scallop and rose ground pattern, page 60.

Method
Work a four plait crossing to introduce leaf and plait pairs at the ringed hole. Work the leaf in the direction of the arrow and introduce pairs for the outer circular plait at a four plait crossing. Two pairs on *a* provide the weaver and outer scallop edge pair. The left hand pairs from the crossing provide the scallop passive pairs. Join in the centre leaf pairs when needed.

Pattern 12

Photograph 140 and pricking 141.

Thread
Fils a Dentelles no. 70. Eight pairs of bobbins.

Reference
Scallop and rose ground pattern, page 60.

Method
At the ringed hole, join in the six pairs with a six plait crossing. The left hand pairs make a leaf to *a*, the other pairs are introduced on the outside edge and the scallop edge is worked. The middle pairs plait

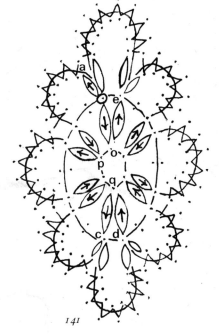

141

with picots around the oval and cross the plait from the scallop. The right hand pairs make a leaf to the centre to *o*, the pin is put between the pairs and a plait is made to *p*. Work is continued to *c* and *q*. At *q*, the pairs make a leaf out to *c*. At *c* a six plait crossing is made, the left hand pairs make a leaf and the scallop and work back to *d*. The other four pairs make a plait to *d* and another six plait crossing is made. The right hand leaf from *d* is hooked into the base of the leaf at *q*. Similarly the plait to *o* is hooked into the base of the leaf before working the leaf to *e*. Four pairs make the plait to the ringed hole. Remember that the outer leaves to *c*, *d* *e* and the ringed hole are made with the scallop passive threads but do not cross the oval plait. The large inner leaves from these points are made with the pairs that work the small centre circle plait.

Pattern 13

Photograph 142 and pricking 143. Suitable for small wall hanging or paperweight.

Thread

Retors D'Alsace no. 30 or mercerized sewing cotton no. 40. Four pairs for the edge trail and four for the inner trail, also six pairs for the leaves and plaits and six for the centre feature.

Method

Begin the inner trail at the ringed hole, also make a six plait crossing as indicated on the pricking, make leaf and plaits. Work the outer edge trail from the pin hole indicated, using the weaver, an edge twisted pair and two cloth pairs. Stop at pin *x*. The two cloth pairs are plaited for a short distance and make a four plait crossing with the plait from the centre. This plait then receives a short plait and becomes the cloth pairs for the next outer curve. On the inner trail pairs are introduced to make leaves *a*, *b* and *c*. As the half stitch centre is worked the weaver is twisted and taken to the trail on the left and back to continue. On the right it must be hooked into the first trail pin worked.

142

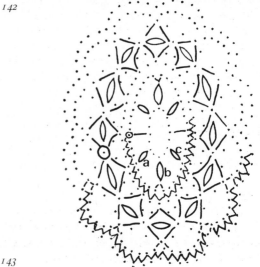

143

84

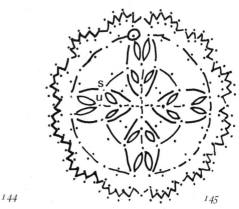

144
145

Pattern 14

Photograph 144 and pricking 145. Suitable for a paperweight.

Thread

Mercerized sewing cotton no. 40. Four pairs in white for the scallop edge, and four for the two centre plaits. Two pairs in colour for each circular plait and leaf feature.

Method

Begin at the ringed hole with a four plait crossing using two white and two coloured pairs. Add the two white pairs on the edge to work the scallop and the other coloured pairs at *s*. At *u* and *v* the extra pairs for the centre plaits are added at four plait crossings. The coloured threads in the photograph facilitate the understanding of this motif (refer to book cover).

Pattern 15

Photograph 146 and pricking 147.

Thread

Retors D'Alsace no. 30 or mercerized sewing cotton no. 40. Four pairs for the plait/leaf edging, four pairs for the trail and eight pairs for the centre leaves. Also four pairs for the plait and plait/leaf feature.

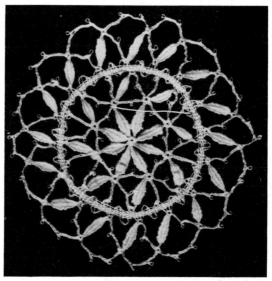

146

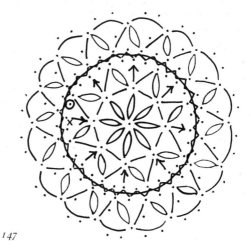

147

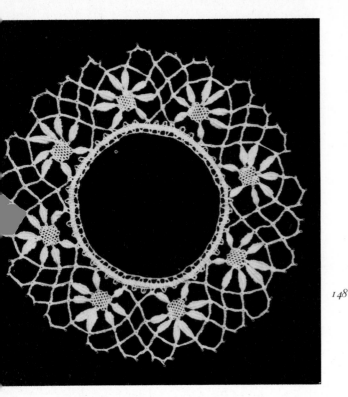

148

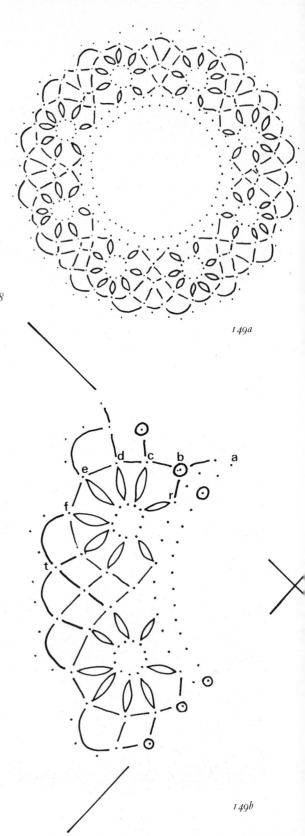

149a

149b

References

Edging, page 48. Six plait crossing, page 57. Eight plait crossing, page 81.

Method

Begin the trail at the ringed dot and immediately join in two pairs for the edge leaf. Two more pairs are added for the plait to work the edge. On the inner side of the trail two pairs are introduced at four points as indicated. The first plait works to *x* and at a six plait crossing joins in four pairs more. The right hand pairs make the centre leaf, the middle pairs make the circular plait and the left hand pairs plait back to the cloth trail. Continue, until four centre leaves are complete, work the eight plait crossing and the other half of the motif.

Pattern 16

Photograph 148 and pricking 149a and b.

Thread

The fine pricking requires Retors D'Alsace no. 50 and the large mat Pearl cotton no. 12. Five pairs for the foot edge and ten for the plaits and leaves.

Method
Prepare the pricking for the large mat by placing eight repeats (four patterns in fig. 149b) around a circle radius 35mm (1⅛ inch). On the footside put two pairs round a pin at *a*, and work through three passive pairs to *b*. Join in two plait pairs, plait introducing two pairs at *c*, *d*, *e*. Continue the footside linking in the plait at *r*, make leaves and work the centre half stitch circle. The pricking indicates where leaves enter the circle, make the remaining leaves and complete mat.

Pattern 17

Photograph 150 and pricking 151. Suitable for the powder compact.

Thread
Mercerized sewing cotton no. 40. Three or four passive pairs and a weaver for each side of the trails that cross. Three passive pairs and a weaver for the inner circular trail. Six pairs for leaves.

References
Braid no. 3, page 66. Tallies, page 33.

Method
Work the braid to understand the method before beginning this motif. Work the crossing trail edging and the inner trail. When the weavers are opposite each other, as indicated, work a tally and continue. As in previous patterns join in pairs to work the three centre leaves, work a six-plait crossing and make the other three leaves.

151

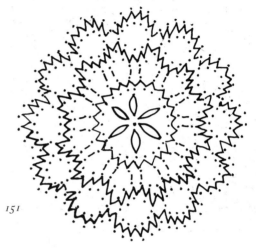

150

152

Pattern 18

Photographs 152 and pricking 153. Suitable for the large trinket box, or without the scallop edge for a powder compact.

Thread
Mercerized sewing cotton no. 40. In white, five pairs for the scallop edge and four for the passives in the trail. In colour, one weaver pair and fourteen pairs for leaves. Two pairs in colour for the stem. Refer to the book cover.

Reference
Scallop braid, page 68.

Method
Practise braid no. 7 before working this motif. Begin the trail at *a* with a weaver and four passive pairs (twisted at the edges and two cloth pairs in the centre). Immediately join in the three passive pairs for the scallop. Hang in one stem pair, hang the second freely on a pin and twist both pairs to meet and work the plait with picots. Continue with the

153

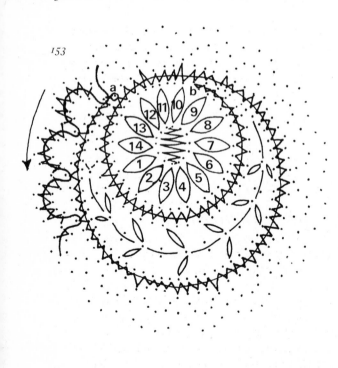

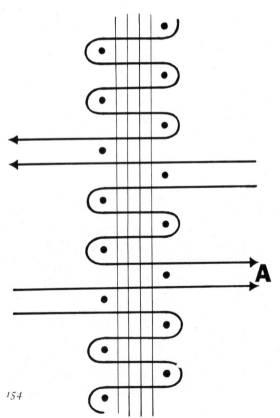

154

outer trail joining in pairs for six leaves. Make the leaves and plait the stem with four plait crossings as necessary. Continue the trail, at *a* the scallop edge is complete. Ignore the fact that leaves *10* to *14* appear to touch the trail. Work the leaves from the stem as required, they are taken through the trail to become the centre leaves. Refer to illus. 154. Leave the weaver on the inner side of the trail immediately before the leaf enters on the outer edge. Put up a pin between the leaf pairs and take the right hand pair straight through with the appropriate stitches. Put in a pin between the weaver and this pair, these are used for the centre leaf. The other pair from the stem leaf also works through the trail and becomes the new weaver. For this reason the trail weaver must be the same colour as the leaves. Continue until six leaves have passed through the trail. Join in the last two coloured pairs for leaf *7*. Work the leaves and the centre half stitch. Work the leaves from the centre as required. Leaves *8* and *9* are taken into the trail and the trail is completed at *b*. Leaves *10* to *14* are hooked into the trail and knotted firmly.

Pattern 19

Photograph 157 and pricking 158. This tie lace should be mounted on fine fabric for a necktie or cravat. Alternatively plaits and leaves are worked afterwards.

Thread
Retors D'Alsace no. 30 or mercerized sewing cotton no. 40. Four pairs for the scallop edge and four for the footside. Two pairs extra are required for the leaves.

References
Braid no. 7, page 68. Rose ground and scallop pattern, page 60.

It is essential to understand the working of these two patterns before making the tie in pattern 19. Note that the footside holes in this pattern have the usual arrangement and if the lace is to be mounted on fabric a straight footside is necessary. If the centre leaf feature is worked, the weaver may be taken round the pin with the usual two twists. Decide on the length of the tie and work one side ignoring the leaves and plaits on the pricking. Continue into the decorative end, introduce two pairs for the leaf and scallop feature at pin *u*. Discard

them at pin *v*. Ignore *a*, *b* and *c* and work the other edging and the other decorative end.

The centre leaf/plait feature
This can be worked when the ends and edgings are complete. Alternatively it can be worked at the same time as the second edge. As work progresses join in pairs for leaves at *a*, *b* and *c*. Make the leaves and join in two pairs extra to make an eight plait crossing. Make four leaves, one goes into the trail at *r* and is discarded. At *p* link in a leaf with the weaver and make another leaf to *z*. Work a long fat leaf direct to *z* and finally link in one leaf at *o* with a hook. Make a leaf to *z* and work a six plait crossing. From *z*, the centre pairs make a leaf and the side pairs plait to the trails, are joined in and then make leaves for the next crossing. Continue.

Pattern 20

Photographs 157 and pricking 158. This tie is more difficult to work than the previous one and the nine pin edge, traditional to Beds-Maltese lace is a new feature.

Thread
As for pattern 19. The nine pin edge requires seven pairs; at the ends additional pairs are used, three for the trail, six for the plait/leaf crossing and two for the small leaves at the bottom of the half stitch circle. The centre plait/leaf feature which is similar to the previous pattern requires six pairs.

Method
Refer to illus. 159. The trail consists of a weaver and two passive pairs. Two pairs are joined in at *a* and plaited to *b* where two new pairs are introduced at a four plait crossing. The right hand pairs plait to *d*, the left hand pairs plait and make picots and eventually arrive at *d* for a four plait crossing. To achieve good picots it is necessary to plait in a straight line and bend the plait round when required for a particular pin. Refer to the pricking and join in one pair extra at each of the capped holes. Divide the trail making two weavers at the centre hole. Work both trails adding pairs at *a*, *b* and *c* for plaits and a leaf. Work these and the six plait crossing. Take the pairs into the trails and out for leaves *1*, *2* and *3*. Join in pairs for leaf *4*. Make the leaves and work the half

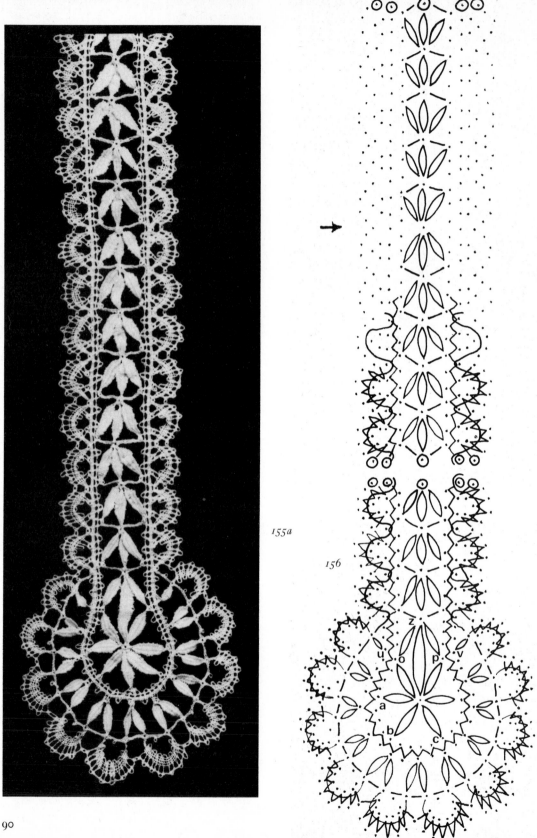

155a

156

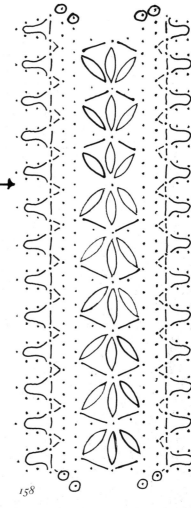

155b

158

157

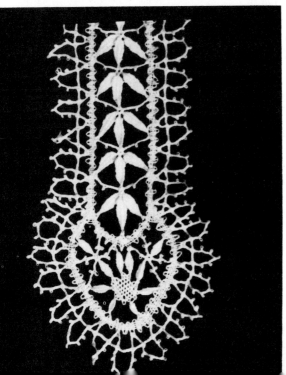

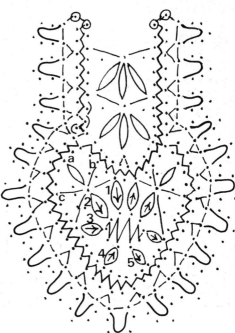

stitch. Leaf 5 is worked, linked to the trail and discarded. Work the trails and centre plaits and join the trails together. One at a time the additional passives are discarded from the cloth trail until two remain for the plaited edging. To discard pairs lay them back and continue the cloth stitch without them. As there are too many pairs for the width of cloth they are very close together, therefore they can be cut off and cannot fray or look unsightly. The centre feature can be added when the edging is complete. Alternatively work as described for the previous pattern.

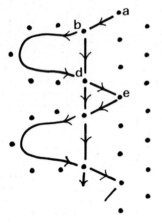

159

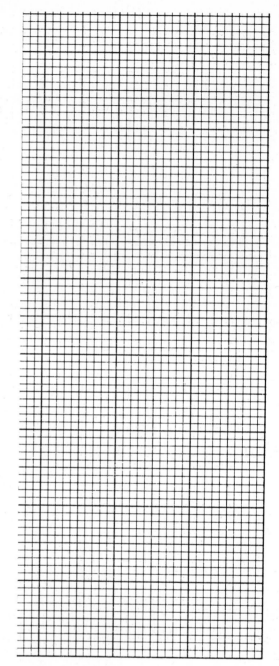

160a

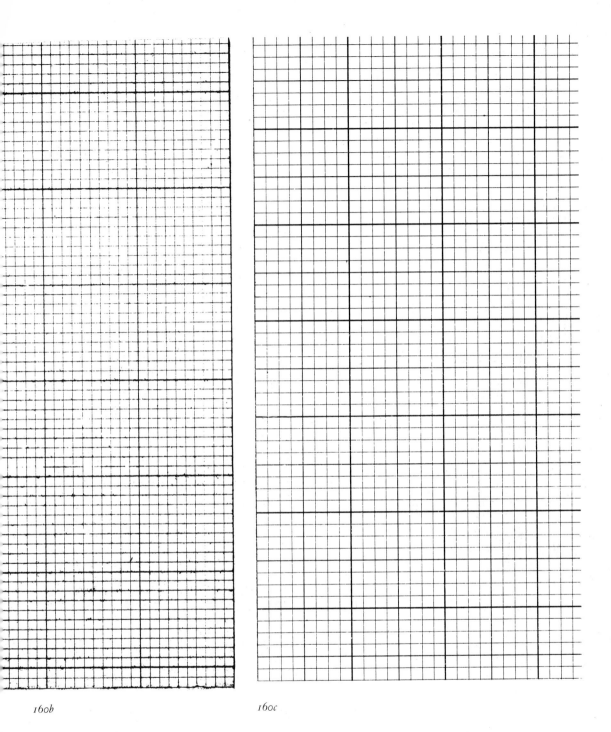

160b
                       160c

List of suppliers

UK

D.J. Hornsby
149 High Street
Burton Latimer
Kettering
Northants
(*All lace making requisites –
mail order service*)

Audrey Sells
49 Pedley Lane
Clifton
Shefford
Beds.
(*All lace making requisites –
mail order service*)

Mace and Nairn
89 Crane Street
Salisbury
Wilts.

T. Brown
Woodside
Greenlands Lane
Prestwood
Great Missenden
Bucks.
(*Bobbin maker*)

B. Phillips
Pantglas
Cellan
Lampeter
Dyfed
(*Bobbin maker*)

D.H. Shaw
47 Zamor Crescent
Thurscroft
Rotherham
S. Yorks.
(*Bobbin maker*)

C. & D. Springett
251 Hillmorton Road
Rugby
Warwicks.
(*Bobbin makers*)

Frank Herring & Sons
27 High West Street
Dorchester
Dorset
DT1 1UP
(*Pillows, bobbins, winders*)

USA

Berga-Ullman, Inc
P.O. Box 918
North Adams, Massachusetts 01247
(*Materials and equipment*)

Frederick J. Fawcett
129 South Street
Boston, Massachusetts 02130
(*Large selection of linen yarns and
threads up to size 140/2*)

Osma G. Tod Studio
319 Mendoza Avenue
Coral Gables, Florida 33134
(*Books, instructions, materials and
equipment*)

Robin and Russ Handweavers
533 N. Adams Street
McMinnville, Oregon 97128
(*Books, materials and equipment*)

Lacis
2990 Adeline Street
Berkeley, California 94703
(*Books, instructions, materials,
equipment and antique laces –
mail order service*)

The Unique and Art Lace Cleaners
5926 Delmar Boulevard
St Louis, Missouri 63112
(*Professional lace cleaning and
restoration*)

Bibliography

Historical information

Bullock, A.M. *Lace and Lacemaking*. Batsford, 1981

Freeman, Charles. *Pillow Lace in the East Midlands.* Luton Museum and Art Gallery, 1958

Head, R.E. *The Lace and Embroidery Collector.* Gale Research Company, Detroit, 1972

Hopewell, G. *Bobbins and Pillow Lace.* Shire Publications

Jackson. *A History of Hand Made Lace.* Gale Research Company, Detroit, 1972

Jourdain, M. *Old Lace.* Gale Research Company, 1981

Van Horrick, M. *Lace: Our Heritage.* Joan Duckworth, 1980

Wardle, P. *Victorian Lace.* Herbert Jenkins, 1968

Wright, Thomas. *The Romance of the Lace Pillow.* Minet, 1971

Practical information

Collier, A. *Creative Design in Bobbin Lace*, Batsford, 1982

Cook and Stott. *The Book of Bobbin Lace Stitches.* Batsford, 1980

Dye, Gillian. *Bobbin Lace Braid*. Batsford, 1979

Luxton, E. *Technique of Honiton Lace*. Batsford, 1979

Maidment, M. *A Manual of Hand Made Bobbin Lace.*

Nottingham, P. *Technique of Bucks Point Lace.* 1976

Nottingham, P. *Technique of Bucks Point Lace.* Batsford, 1981

Nottingham, P. *Technique of Torchon Lace.* Batsford, 1979

Index